M000032197

GENUINE

MIRACLES

Javier,

Thank you so much for being part of this project! May God continue to make Himself known through your miracle! And may you always remember that He has you here for a reason, to do good works that He has already set out for you!

—

GENUINE

MIRACLES

true stories from real people

LEE FREEMAN

GENUINE MIRACLES

Copyright © 2018 by Lee Freeman.

All rights reserved. Printed in the United States of America. No part of this book may be used or reproduced in any manner whatsoever without written permission except in the case of brief quotations embodied in critical articles or reviews.

This book is a work of non-fiction. Although some names have been changed to protect the identities of some interviewees, the stories are true. Some emotional accounts and unimportant details have been artistically represented by the author, but every attempt has been made to accurately represent the events herein according to how they actually transpired. All interviewees signed an affidavit of authenticity confirming that their stories are true.

There is no way to guarantee you will experience a miracle. This book recommends following Jesus, praying, and having faith. When you experience hardships, which the Bible guarantees will happen, the author and the publisher will not be held responsible.

For information contact :
Genuine Miracles
GenuineMiracles@Gmail.com
(904) TRUE - GOD
www.GenuineMiracles.com

Book and Cover design by Lee Freeman
ISBN: 978-1-73266-680-1

First Edition: November 2018

This book is dedicated to skeptics and those whose mainstream intelligence has disallowed them from believing in the supernatural. May this book challenge what you have previously known and inspire you to seek answers outside of where you have previously found them. (Hint: start with Jesus)

Some people's names have been changed, but all of the following events are told as they happened. All interviewees signed an affidavit verifying the authenticity of their stories.

CONTENTS

CHAPTER ONE

Disappointment

G od is romantic.

When I was in high school, my best friend and I used to work together to come up with elaborate "Promposals," except we did not just do it for Prom – we did it for all sorts of other dances and events. We came up with grand schemes to make 100-foot signs, fill cars with balloons, make scavenger hunts, etc. No plan was too extravagant.

We loved doing this because we are romantics and creators by nature. The best part of it, though, was how it made the girl feel: a little bit embarrassed maybe, but special. All of this was done for her. She was the object of special affection. It took incredible time, energy, intention, and planning.

I did not realize it at the time, but I was doing that because I was made in the image of my romantic Creator. He does the same thing, but on a stellar scale. He will move Heaven and Earth to say *I love you*. To the Creator, to the One who composed the cosmos, no plan is too extravagant. No proposal is too personalized. Of course, He sometimes prefers smaller gestures of love instead. Just as there is no one-size-fits-all perfect proposal, God customizes His romance for each of us because He knows and loves each of us individually.

What This Book Is

I am a skeptic. Sometimes, I am even a cynic. I have met plenty of Christians who think it is a miracle every time a flower blooms or the sun rises. When they say things like that, I think, *gag me with a spoon.* Sure, God made the flower to bloom and the sun to rise, and he made them beautiful for our enjoyment, but...a *miracle*? I do not use that term lightly.

Growing up, I loved to read about the miracles in the Bible: Daniel and the lions' den, feeding the 5,000, raising Lazarus from the dead, healing the centurion's son, making the blind see. However, I did not see any miracles in my world – until it happened. God made a miracle for me. After that, I started looking harder and listening more carefully.

I began hearing more and more stories of real miracles happening to people I knew. Not always on the scale of resurrection or feeding thousands of people with one kid's lunch box, but still mind-blowing, chill-down-your-spine, make-you-want-to-cry stories.

I also heard many stories that changed the lives of the people telling them but did not compel me. You know, like, "I had a dream about my daughter getting married to a nice Christian man, and it really gave me a lot of peace. Two years later, she *did* marry a nice Christian man. It's a miracle!" Those are the kinds of stories I did not include in this book. I am grateful for those stories, but this book only includes stories I think will be compelling for others.

This book is comprised of stories I believe. I have interviewed all of the people whose stories appear here and had them sign an affidavit confirming their stories actually happened. This is non-fiction. This is not a collection of fairy tales to make you feel good. These are not elaborations. They are true stories of a real God interacting with and interceding for actual people.

This Book is Disappointing

If you subscribe to the Genuine Miracles YouTube channel, you will hear the stories straight from the mouths of those who experienced them. However, without actually meeting them face to face, I think it is impossible to grasp the emotional magnitude of the miracles these people have experienced.

As I approach miracle interviews now, I have come to expect a certain enigmatic expression nearly all of the interviewees share. Especially as the conversation begins, I see in their eyes a desperate hope that their listener will understand not only the improbability of what happened, but also the more important fire that was ignited in their souls as a result. Not only the cataclysmic 'coincidences' that led to the miracles, but the unshakeable assurance they will carry with them until they meet their Maker.

Speaking from personal experience and from over twenty interviews so far, the greatest frustration in having experienced a miracle is the impossibility of conferring its full transformative power onto another person. It is like being in love: everyone knows it is good, everyone wants it to happen, but no one can know its rapture without being in the embrace. In that sense, this book is disappointing. However, I encourage you to search these interviewees' eyes, in the portraits enclosed and in their YouTube interviews. See the gratitude of a mother who has been provided sustenance for her beloved children. See the joy of a prisoner who has been relieved of his captivity. See the craving in their eyes to share an unbelievable story that has changed the way they see *everything*.

The Danger of This Book

Take your time on this section; it is one of the most important parts of this book, and many people will find it the most challenging.

One of the easiest lies to walk away from this book believing is that God's answer is always *yes*. It is not. This is mostly a book of *yes*es, but God's answer is often *no* or *not yet*. Sometimes a *no* sets us up for a miracle greater than what we hoped for. Sometimes a *no* is the end of a chapter or even the end of a book.

That harsh reality is one of the most common reasons people turn away from God. However, let us explore the implications of a God who always says *yes*. For a comedic version, watch *Bruce Almighty*. For a more sobering reality, contemplate it for a moment. If the answer to our prayers is always *yes,* God becomes an omnipotent vending machine, bending to our wills. Since we control God, this essentially makes us God, but with some terrifying defects:

> 1. We are not perfect. If you do not have a working picture of the calamity caused by cosmic power in sinful hands, take a look at the 'divine' dysfunction of Greek mythology.

7

2. We are not omniscient. We cannot see the entire continuum of time like God can. He sees how one incident will affect outcomes a century from now. We often see only our current pain.

The real God, however, is perfect; he is omniscient. Although it is incredibly difficult at times, I am grateful His ways are higher than mine. The ideal God should know more than I do. He should tell me *no* sometimes. Most importantly, he should be loving, and I am so glad He is. Think about it: would a loving parent always say *yes*? Are there even times when a child's intentions are pure and selfless but the answer should still be *no*? As humbling as it is, we must realize that compared to our omniscient God, we are but children in perspective. Our loving Father still hears our pleas, and our pain grieves His heart, but sometimes the most loving thing a father can do is let His beloved child experience pain.

When the answer is *no*, it does not mean God did not hear. It does not mean God does not care. Sometimes, until we reach Heaven, we will never learn why the answer was *no*. That can feel impossible to justify and understand. In those times, try to remember Romans 8:28 – "God works all things together for the good of those who love Him." Pray that God would help you to accept His answer, and stay close to Him.

Having gone through several seasons when God did not intervene in a crisis the way I thought He should have, I can testify there are many times I am grateful He did not do what I was asking. I have a feeling when I reach Heaven and get more perspective, though, I am going to end up being grateful for *all* of the times when the answer was *no*.

The Challenge

Most likely, you will read some of these stories and find them challenging to believe. They defy conventional logic. They confound possibility. Nevertheless, these stories are told by the people who experienced them, real people who were not paid, people whose lives have been shaped by these miracles. I have known most of them for years; they are trusted, respected, longtime members of their communities. Not only that, but I met almost all of these people in my hometown! This book is but a drop in the ocean of people who are alive today who have experienced miracles!

Skeptics, why would these people lie? Why would they hold so resolutely to something that makes no sense? What do they have to gain from holding an unpopular opinion? Why would so many people I know claim to have experienced the supernatural firsthand? All of these people told their stories before they heard about this project – except for one that was happening while this project was starting – so I know they did not share their stories so they could be in a book!

Christians, do you really believe in an omnipotent God? Do you *really*? Do you believe He is alive today and He cares about each of us, interacting with us and intervening in our lives? Do you believe in the power of prayer? Do you believe God is good?

Belief is often limited by past experiences. Will your history limit your destiny? Will you truncate your transformation because the calculations do not compute? Consider: can the God of the Bible do miracles new and different from what He did in the Bible? Can God speak to people on Earth, either through an audible voice or through an inner prompting? Can God work outside the boundaries of modern science and medicine? If you answered *no* to any of those questions, I challenge you to check your answers against the Bible. If you answered *yes*, remember that as you read these stories.

If you are unsure about your responses to any of those questions, I encourage you to keep your mind open as you read. The God who created the bounds of possibility is surely able to break them.

How to Use This Book

If you are a skeptic, read on and test your skepticism against these eye witness testimonies. If you are a Christian in crisis, read on and find encouragement. If you are neither, read on and be amazed.

Regardless of whether you are a skeptic, a Christian, or both, your faith will probably be stretched in the following pages. However, this book should not be the end of your journey. It should get you started. Think: why did Jesus perform miracles? The miracles were never the end. He performed miracles to get people curious about Him. This book points to Jesus.

I hope you will seek answers for the questions which this book generates. The best two sources for answers are the Bible and prayer. Beyond that, I recommend finding a Bible-believing church and Bible-believing mentors to help you navigate these difficult questions.

My prayer is that God uses this book to stir your heart. I pray you would come to a greater realization of how incredible yet tangible God's love is for you. I pray this book would help you to fall more deeply in love with God. May that motivate you to live a life sold out for Him, striving to glorify Him and love radically so you may reveal Him to others. Amen.

CHAPTER TWO

God Changes Soles

I'm Lee, and this is my true story.

I grew up in a Christian home, always having an understanding of who God is. My family loved me and did a wonderful job of teaching me to view the world in light of God's truth. I had a good sense of God's general love for mankind: "For God so loved the world that he gave His one and only son, that whoever believes in Him should not perish but have eternal life" (John 3:16, NIV). To do that, God must have really loved the world. I did not yet realize how much He loved *me*.

Part of the reason I felt unloved is that I grew up in a dangerous neighborhood in the inner city. I was a racial minority in my school, and I was often excluded as a result. On top of that, my parents thought since I was a boy, I would think it was embarrassing if they told me they loved me, so they stopped saying it for a while. This was all happening during puberty, and to make matters worse, I was becoming keenly aware of my sinful nature and the fact that no matter how hard I tried, I kept screwing up.

While I was wrestling with all of that, my father's company underwent a restructuring. The job my father had kept for over 10 years was suddenly gone; he had the choice to take a different job that did not interest him or take a severance package. My parents took it as an answer to prayer – they had wanted to move to Colorado for years. I took it as the end of the world.

The move to Colorado turned out to be more difficult than anticipated. We struggled financially. Hearing my parents talk about their financial stresses, I tried to avoid adding any burdens that would make matters worse. In hindsight, it was not my role to be worried about this, and my parents always provided everything I needed. However, what a child thinks he needs and what he actually needs are often different things. Moreover, children often adopt their parents' worries. I was no exception.

Unfortunately, my shoes were disintegrating. I only had one pair, and the soles were separating from the uppers. My shoes had several other holes, and they were hurting my feet, partly because my feet were getting too big for them. My shoes were a 9 or 9.5, but my feet were easily a 10. Worst of all, the appearance of my shoes made me a regular target of ridicule at school, where I was trying to make a good impression on my new peers.

I eventually had to ask my parents for new shoes. When I did, their response was disheartening: "I'm sorry, Lee, we just don't have the money right now. We're going to have to wait a little bit." It probably would not have been as long as it seemed, but I was unduly pessimistic. Even though in retrospect, it was not an emergency, it felt like one to me. I started getting emotional.

Then my mother said something amazing, offering a glimmer of hope: "Let's pray for new shoes." So we did. We huddled in the living room and prayed that God would provide new shoes. My parents and I were the only ones who knew about that prayer, aside from God. We did not tell anyone.

The next day, a family friend showed up at the door, unannounced, with a box in his hand. He asked my mom, "Hey, do you have anyone who wears a size 10.5 and could use a pair of shoes? Grandma sent us these, but they don't fit any of our kids." They were brand name, nicer than any shoes I had ever had in my life. They fit perfectly. I wore them every day for over a year, and they remain the most comfortable shoes I have ever owned.

That miracle means a lot more to me than comfortable shoes, though. It means God loves me personally. He was grieved by my hurting heart, and He wanted to send me an extravagant gesture of His love. God loves not just the *world* – He loves *me*. He loves *you*.

Over a decade later, I shared that story with about ten church friends. In response, two or three others shared their miracle stories. Dodie's and Robin's stories, found in the pages ahead, were among them. I felt the Holy Spirit wash over me with a tangibility I have seldom experienced before and a divine prompting that was as clear as any in my life: *Lee, I want you to share these stories with the world.*

Hence, this project was born.

CHAPTER THREE

Radiant Love

I'm Jay, and this is my true story.

Jay

When I was five years old, my family moved from a suburb of Denver, Colorado to Los Angeles, California. The circumstances of our move meant we had to leave fairly suddenly. We left most of our belongings behind and even traded vehicles with a family in our church because theirs was bigger.

We departed early on a summer morning in 1983. My father, the patriarch of our family, had planned to make the entire drive in one day. My mother had packed accordingly, loading the car with snacks and gallon jugs of water, the ones that look like milk jugs. We had to be strategic though. Every spot occupied by a snack meant one more belonging that we had to leave behind.

I slept during most of the trip, but I woke up and looked around as we passed through Las Vegas, where I had been born. While we traveled through Las Vegas, my mother told me about an upcoming stretch of the trip, the Mojave Desert and Death Valley, which has an average annual rainfall of less than two inches. Even as a young child, I found it fascinating we would be visiting the driest place in North America.

As we entered the desert, a cloudless sky mercilessly radiated heat. Eventually, the sweltering heat overpowered our vehicle; the engine sputtered and stopped. We rolled to a halt on the side of the road in an open patch of desert. My father popped the hood and tried to assess the situation. Even though he had little to no experience working on cars, he figured our car had overheated. Desperate, he took the last of our drinking water and poured it into the radiator. The car begrudgingly started, and we were able to travel a small distance down the road.

But the car died again. As the engine chugged to a stop, a profound silence settled on us. My father got out and looked around. No call boxes, no buildings, no cars in sight. I was too young to realize it at the time, but the situation was dire. We were stranded on a blazing summer day in the middle of the desert with no water and little food. We had no way out.

Helpless, my father busied himself under the hood. He knew with more water, he could cool the radiator, but there was no water left. My mother, no less desperate, had a different solution. She gathered my siblings and me next to the car and told us we needed to pray for rain. Overhearing her, my father scoffed. He was frustrated at the ridiculous idea. There was not a cloud in the sky, and we were in Death Valley. Nevertheless, my mother persisted.

We prayed for what felt like a long time. No rain. Undeterred, my mother left us for a moment and pleaded with my father to join us. We needed to pray as a family, she argued. My father had nothing he could do anyway, so he eventually relented.

We prayed for a moment or two. I felt the small prick of something cold hitting my skin. My family felt it, too. It could not be true. By the time we all opened our eyes, it was a downpour. We looked around in amazement; the desert surrounding us remained bright and dry. It was only raining right over and around our car. The rain was torrential now – huge, cold drops. We scrambled to grab the empty gallon jugs and put them out. Despite the tiny openings, they were filling up. I can almost picture God sitting in Heaven, aiming drops right where we needed them.

My father tried to retrieve his jaw from the drenched desert floor. My mother's smile was as bright as the sun. Once the jugs were full, the rain stopped. With plenty of water to spare, my father bathed the car's radiator with the cold rainwater, and we were able to make it to a rest stop.

When we arrived in California, my parents could not stop talking about our miracle. In fact, it revolutionized my father's faith – rather, it sparked his faith. He had been 'playing Christian' to court and then appease my mother, but his faith was inauthentic. The rain changed that. God changed that. We had all experienced firsthand His love and power. The rest of my childhood was marked by church, family devotionals, lots of prayer, and an unshakable family faith. With Dad leading the way.

CHAPTER FOUR

God Has Your Back

I'm Manny, and this is my true story.

Manny

S hortly after I graduated college, I was hurt in a car accident; my back was injured and my ribs were cracked. Daily tasks were difficult for a while, but I was careful during my recovery. Over the next couple of months, it seemed to fully heal, and I began to ease back into normalcy.

In August, a good friend of mine who was a youth pastor asked me to help him at a church camp, and I quickly agreed. I have a heart for reaching young people and helping to introduce them to God; I was excited for this opportunity.

On the second-to-last day of the camp, there was a tug of war contest between the different churches in attendance. Being a competitive guy, I eagerly joined our youth group on the battlefield. As the whistle blew, I applied my full strength to the task. Suddenly, I was overcome with pain. Collapsing, I realized I had re-injured my back.

I spent the next several hours alone in my room, in immense pain. I stared at the ceiling and tried not to move, hoping the pain would subside. From my bed, though, I could hear music. The evening worship service was starting. I decided I could either be in my room in pain or with my group in pain, so I hobbled down to the service.

The service was moving. I could tell God was at work in the hearts of the teens there. In spite of the pain in my back, I remembered why I had come. Looking around at our group, I saw an opportunity to engage with two students. They were young in their faith, but I could tell they wanted more.

I began to encourage them and talk with them about God's plan for their lives and how much He loves them. I put my arms around their shoulders and began to pray for them. As I was praying, I became aware of the youth pastor's presence behind me. He placed his hands on my back and began to pray. I was focused on the students, and I assumed my friend was simply praying along with me.

Suddenly, he ran his hand up my back. I felt a strong heat, unlike anything his hands could produce. The pain in my back was instantly and permanently gone.

Afterward, I learned he had been praying for the healing of my back. I had no idea at the time, though, so the healing came as a complete surprise. Skeptics sometimes hear stories of miraculous healings and dismiss them as the placebo effect or the power of the mind. In my case, however, the healing prayer happened without my knowledge. All I knew at the time was that I was no longer hurting.

Although I had been in immense pain, my injury was not life-threatening. If God had not healed me when He did, I would have been fine. It would have affected me for a while, but I would have recovered eventually. However, God is a loving father. He knows me as an individual, and it grieved Him that I was in pain.

Throughout my life since, that moment of healing has served as a landmark of my faith. In difficulty and times when I have doubts, I cannot deny the God of the universe knows and loves each of His children deeply and personally.

CHAPTER FIVE

Dimension

I'm Paula, and this is my true story.

Paula

When I was eleven years old, my ten-year-old brother Steve was killed in a car accident, leaving behind my parents, my sister, my older brother, and me. Steve's passing was devastating to our family. As painful as it was, my brother's death somehow strengthened my faith. In fact, after Steve went to Heaven, I felt like he was watching over me. Every time I was in trouble, I imagined, he would pull God's sleeve to get His attention and yell, "Dad, Paula's in trouble! You've got to help her out!"

As I got older, I learned God was just as concerned about me as Steve was. He did not need my brother to pull on his sleeve. Not one sparrow falls without His knowledge, and the Bible says I am worth far more than a sparrow (Matthew 10:29-31). On a fateful trip to Port Austin, Michigan, God proved that to me in an unbelievable way.

***

My family owned a little cabin right on the shore of Lake Huron. The cabin was a magical place, a place that seemed like a little slice of Heaven. Time did not exist. Cares were gone. The whole world was ours, made for our enjoyment. Most importantly, it was all about family. We spent our time talking, laughing, or playing together outside – it did not matter, as long as we were together.

When I was back in the real world, I often let my mind drift back over the snowbanked hills to our cabin at the lake's edge. I longed for the cabin when I was not there, so when my family told me we would be meeting for a weekend in the winter of 1984, I could hardly contain my excitement.

My sister Sarah and I lived in the Detroit area and planned to make the 100-mile drive after work on a Thursday evening. There was only one highway leading to our destination, and it had only one lane in each direction. Because of this, the highway was constantly busy, a frustrating drive. At least riding together made it much more enjoyable.

We loaded my 1979 Dodge Aspen after work as darkness fell. As we were about to depart, we heard an announcement on the radio warning us of poor driving conditions due to freezing rain. This was common in Michigan winters. The roads seemed fine, though, so we paid little attention to it and began on our way.

Sarah and I were talking and laughing as we made our way up Highway 53. Even though traffic was thick, it was moving well. The driver right behind me, the driver right in front of me, and I all seemed content to be going about 55 miles per hour – slow enough for the conditions (we still had not encountered any ice), but fast enough to feel like we were making good progress. The constant stream of drivers in the southbound lane seemed to be doing about the same.

Then with no warning, I hit black ice, and we began to spin.

The oncoming headlights became blurred, horizontal streaks of light and my adrenaline surged. "Take your hands off the wheel," Sarah said. "It's in God's hands now." I was sure we were going to die.

It was eerily quiet as we spun several times. We heard the muffled impact of our car bouncing off something relatively soft, a snowbank. We made a few more rotations and then with a bang, came to an abrupt halt. Utter silence.

We breathed out and lifted our heads slowly. "Are we dead?" I asked.

"I don't know," Sarah said, "pinch me." I did. "Ow! I don't think so!"

"Pinch me!" I said. She did. "Ow! I felt that, too – I think we're both alive!" Somehow, we were both uninjured.

I noticed our dog, Mia, who had been in the back seat before we started to spin, was now sitting on the floor in front of my sister. Mia looked up at us inquisitively.

I glanced outside and noticed something shocking. "Where did all the traffic go?" I gasped.

"I thought we were going to die! There was traffic coming in both directions," Sarah said. "How are we still alive?" There were no cars within sight.

We got out to assess the situation and were astonished to find there was no damage to the car. We could see the path our vehicle had taken, careening through the median and spewing snow all over the road. A rear tire was now lodged in a snowbank, the car facing the wrong way in the southbound shoulder. Sarah tried kicking the snow around the tire, to no avail.

As we looked around, we noticed the only visible light was a small farmhouse in the distance. Sarah suggested walking to it for help, but there was at least a foot of snow. "No, you'll freeze to death," I said, "Let's just wait in the car to see if someone comes along."

Sure enough, after a few minutes of waiting in the car, we saw headlights. It turned out to be an old, beat-up pickup truck, slowing as it passed us. We heard its loud idle, choking and sputtering. I could see a man driving and a woman in the passenger seat holding a baby. The truck stopped in the middle of the road just ahead of our vehicle. The driver did not pull over, just stopped in the middle of the road like he owned it. The man got out. "Are you stuck?" he asked.

"Yeah, can you help us?"

"I have a shovel in the back of the truck. Let me see if I can dig you out," he said.

We walked around to the back of our car and watched as he started to dig. After only a few strokes of the shovel, we noticed another set of headlights coming toward us. It turned out to be a state trooper. As he emerged from his vehicle, his humongous frame came into view; he was one of the largest people I have ever seen. Very tall, lean, muscular. "Hello," I said.

"Hey," he grinned, "Did you make this mess out in the road?"

"Yeah," I admitted, "Sorry about that."

"No, it's okay." His face grew earnest, "Is everyone okay?"

"Yeah, everyone is okay."

"So, you're stuck?" he asked.

"Yes, but this nice gentleman..." I gestured behind me and paused.

"What gentleman?" He asked.

"Sarah, what happened to that guy?"

"I have no idea," she said, "I was watching the state trooper pull up." The man with the truck had somehow vanished without either of us noticing.

The state trooper seemed unconcerned. "Alright, what I want you to do is get in your car, and when I tell you to gun it, gun it!" He strolled to the rear of the car, and we got inside, rolling down the front windows so we could hear the trooper.

"Okay," he yelled as *he lifted the rear of the car off the ground and out of the snowbank*, "Gun it!"

In disbelief, I looked down at the speedometer and hit the gas pedal. We surged forward. Almost immediately, Sarah exclaimed, "Paula, look!"

I hit the brakes, looked up, and saw a wall of traffic going in both directions. There was another state trooper, one I had not seen seconds before, standing in the middle of the road, holding a flare and directing traffic.

As I tried to make sense of it, I was startled by the state trooper who had helped us out of the snowbank. He was suddenly at my window and announced with a huge smile, "Okay, you're all set!"

"How did you do that?" I asked, astounded.

"Just a little bit of muscle, that's all," he grinned. "You be safe, and have a great weekend." He let us turn around, and we were off.

***

I cannot explain what happened that night except for this: if my sister and I had died as we thought we would, my parents would have survived three of their children. I cannot imagine the pain that would cause them. God protected us that night because He loves us and our family, and He has a plan for our lives.

Not a sparrow falls without Him knowing. More importantly, He has the power to catch the sparrow and protect it from harm. We are His children, and He loves us immeasurably more than sparrows.

CHAPTER SIX

Labor of Love

By Jennifer Hutchins

I'm Jennifer, and this is my true story.

Jennifer

Shortly after I met my husband, we were on one of those long, romantic, talk-about-everything-under-the-sun walks common with new relationships. We stumbled on to the topic of worst fears. I answered (honestly) that my worst fear was having a disabled child.

Much of my life to that point had been geared toward worldly success and high performance standards. I left home at seventeen, finished college at twenty, and completed graduate school at twenty-one. I was in a career where my peers were a decade my senior. I had money, no debt, freedom, and respect in my field. I felt immense horror at the prospect of having a child who could never live up to the standards I held so precious and worked so hard to maintain.

My husband and I married soon after that fateful walk and continued our adventurous and mostly carefree lifestyle. We bought our first home together at twenty-two in a small, prestigious resort community in the Utah mountains. We traveled frequently and saw places most people only dream of visiting. We stayed in luxury hotels, ate at the best restaurants, and spent more hours than we could count shopping for whatever we wanted just because we could.

A few years into our marriage, I became pregnant. Other than a few months of morning sickness, things went smoothly. For the rest of my pregnancy, I felt great. I constantly received compliments about how tiny and cute my baby bump was. I wore beautiful maternity clothes, many of the same clothes Kate Middleton wore during her first pregnancy, and I was still wearing four-inch stilettos well into my ninth month. Time after time, my test results were exceptional. No abnormalities, no cause for concern, nothing but perfect health for me and the baby in every way.

Three weeks before my due date, I was at work when I realized I had not felt the baby kick for a few hours. I called my doctor, and she sent me in to the hospital to have a non-stress test to check for fetal movement. My husband met me at the hospital, and I spent several tense hours hooked up to a fetal monitor and ultrasound machine. Thankfully, the baby was still alive and moved with a bit of stimulation. While there was no immediate cause for concern, the doctor told us, we had an important choice to make: I could either sit in a hospital bed hooked up to monitors until my due date, or I could be induced that day.

We moved upstairs to labor and delivery, and they began to attempt to induce me. They started me on a very low dose of oxytocin to attempt to jumpstart my labor. I stayed awake through the night, in low but constant pain from the medicine. By the next morning, I was still no closer to having my baby. Mostly I was just nauseous, tired, and anxious.

My doctor came in early that morning and explained they were planning on giving me a much larger dose of oxytocin, one that would most certainly shock my body into labor. She explained that at thirty-seven weeks, the baby was full term; the forced labor would be fine for the baby and me. As we sat there talking to the doctor, I heard a clear voice in my mind.

You need to ask for a C-section.

I nearly jumped in surprise at the intensity of the thought. It did not make sense though, and I ignored it.

Instead, I continued making plans with the doctor to induce labor. Again, the thought came that I needed a C-section, this time louder and more insistent.

I mentioned the idea to my doctor. She and my husband were equally confused and concerned at my suggestion. All medical knowledge points to avoiding C-sections if possible. They increase the risk of complications, likelihood of infection, and length of recovery. They are much more expensive, require more doctors for the procedure, and take up operating rooms. Long term, C-sections increase the risk of complications during future pregnancies as well.

Both my doctor and my husband spent several minutes trying to talk me out of having an unnecessary C-section. The voice in my mind grew more insistent and more firm. As my doctor was telling me I was being unreasonable, I said a quick prayer to God, asking to know if I was making the right decision. I immediately had a peace wash over me, a confirmation the decision was right and was necessary for my safety and the safety of my baby.

My doctor finally relented, and after she left the room, I confided to my husband the experience I had just had. While he was still nervous about a seemingly unnecessary surgery, he trusted me and he trusted God. He decided to support me in my unorthodox decision.

The surgery went smoothly that evening, and five minutes into it, my son came into the world. After surgery, we spent a few hours of bliss holding our newborn. For a short time in the quiet hours of early morning, my husband and I marveled privately at our perfect little gift.

Early the next morning, the pediatrician brought our baby back from the nursery and said he needed to discuss something with us. He looked me straight in the eye and without hesitation said, "Your baby has symptoms consistent with Down syndrome."

My world came crashing down.

He kept speaking to us, describing the long-term concerns, our son's outlook, and tests that needed to be done immediately. I barely heard a word. Instead, pictures flashed through my mind. Images of wheelchair-bound, deformed children covered in drool. Images of short busses and bullying and burying my child in a tiny grave. My fear of the future began to overwhelm me.

Friends and family came to the hospital to visit our baby, and I had my husband send them away with no explanation. I was ashamed, embarrassed, and heartbroken. My perfect world and my perfect family had been shattered, and I did not know how to pick up the pieces.

I began praying fervently to understand, to have comfort, even to have all of this be a mistake, a misdiagnosis. Anything to take away the pain. Anything to bring hope back to my soul. My husband had to return to work, and I spent many lonely hours sitting in a hospital room with my sleeping newborn, wondering how I would continue living my life.

During one of these lonely afternoons, my doctor came to visit me. She had reviewed our son's test results, and she made a shocking confession. She told me my son would not have survived labor. While everything had looked perfect on the ultrasound the day of his birth, she now could see he had a heart defect. The defect was mild and was not dangerous long-term, but the stress of labor would have been too much for my baby.

Best case scenario, we would have ended up in an emergency C-section after many hours of hard labor and with both of us in distress. Worst case scenario, and probably more likely, my baby would have died. She apologized profusely for questioning my decision. All of the best information available had pointed to a textbook perfect induction and labor, and yet I had somehow known exactly what we really needed. She was amazed and confused. "How did you know?"

I smiled at her sheepishly. "I'm pretty sure God told me."

She nodded once and responded, "It seems like He did."

A feeling of peace and comfort fell over me. As I looked at my sweet son, I finally saw what I was supposed to see all along: perfection. As I told the doctor the truth, I realized God had saved my son. God was in the details of my life. He had a plan for me, and a plan for my family. I did not know what exactly God had in store for us, but if He felt it necessary to intercede to keep Ethan alive, then His placement of a child like Ethan with our family was purposeful and divine.

As the weeks passed, in times of darkness and grief, I recalled the moment in the hospital when I realized God had saved Ethan, and I was comforted. We learned more about having a child with Down syndrome, a widely misunderstood condition. The information was equal parts hopeful and overwhelming. The amount of care a child like Ethan needs is monumental, but if the care is given, the quality of life can be marvelous.

Ethan is almost four now. Our lives had changed dramatically. I left my career, with its clout and prestige and money, to care for my son full-time. I have traded in my power suits and mani-pedis for yoga pants and a messy bun. Instead of getting fulfillment from praise and recognition and bonuses, my heart fills with joy when tiny hands clasp onto my neck and tiny lips give me slobbery kisses. His successes are my successes, and his happiness is my happiness. Ethan has taught me that the world's definition of success is different from God's definition, and God's success is the type that will make us truly happy.

Of course, we still go through difficult times. My life is dictated by doctor appointments, feeding issues, and prescription refills. There is stress and grief and fear every time I see my son strapped to yet another machine. But we see small miracles every day, too. My husband is blessed with a job that provides plenty of income. Our money is no longer a symbol of our status, but a tool we gratefully use to provide Ethan with what he needs to fulfill his potential.

While a lot has changed, a lot is still the same. We still travel frequently, with Ethan in tow. Most recently, we took him sailing. He sat near the stern of the boat, buckled firmly in his life jacket, and laughed with glee as the wind off the ocean rustled his hair.

We have learned to adapt our family hobbies to include him. Ethan routinely hikes a mile or so up the trail on his own steam, picking up rocks and branches along the way. When he tires, he rides in a backpack that my husband carries, and he waves enthusiastically to all who pass.

Ethan climbs all over everything, and now that he has grown taller, nothing is safe from his grabby little hands. He rides horses and plays catch and dances to music. He plays with friends and runs errands with mommy and loves being the center of attention. He has his dad's eyes and energy, and my love of books and music. In short, he is the son I always imagined I would have.

I often think back to that day in the hospital, to those words that pounded so insistently in my head until I accepted them for the miracle they were. I will be forever grateful that God enabled me to save my son. I will also be forever grateful that, in spite of my own misguided fears and human failings, God loved me enough to send a special child that would end up saving me from myself.

I used to chase the world's idea of perfection – money, success, image, and power. Now I chase God's idea of perfection – love, acceptance, faith, and service to those in need.

Jennifer has left her traditional career to pursue a career as a writer of young adult and middle grade fiction. See more of her work and follow her at JenHutchins.com.

CHAPTER SEVEN

Milk

I'm Jennissa, and this is my true story.

Jennissa

One evening, I was driving home in Los Angeles after a convicting church service. The message that night had been about hearing God's voice. The thought excited me – I wanted to be one of God's messengers, going where He needs me and doing His work. As I was driving, I prayed, "God, I want to hear your voice."

Immediately, I felt Him say, "Okay, exit right here. Go to the grocery store, and buy milk." I was stunned. It was like He had just been waiting for me to ask. Also, I do not even drink milk, so it was a strange directive to say the least.

I thought I might just be imagining it, but I figured, *what do I have to lose? Worst case scenario, I'll just have milk at home. Someone will drink it!* Plus, I had just prayed asking God to speak to me, so I figured I should give it a shot.

I took the exit and realized I was entering an unfamiliar part of town. There was graffiti decorating the transformer boxes and fire hydrants, litter filling the gutters. Small, disheveled houses jostled against one another for space. Some of them were vacant skeletons, as if the life had been squeezed out of them. Despite my discomfort, I pressed on, found the grocery store, and bought a gallon of milk.

I dodged a pothole as I exited the parking lot. Suddenly, I heard the prompting again: "Take the milk to the house with the lights on." I peered down the street ahead of me. All of the houses on both sides had their lights off except for one.

Before approaching the house, I sat in my car in the darkness. My stomach fluttered. My pulse quickened. *This person is going to think I'm such a freak! There's no way God told me this! This can't be real. Who knows who will open that door? I should just leave…*

I took a deep breath. Again, I remembered my prayer. *I asked for this. I have to do it!* I tentatively walked up to the door and knocked. As footsteps approached on the other side of the door, I heard a baby's scream. A woman's face greeted me. She looked exhausted, crazed almost. Her eyes told me she had been crying. She held an inconsolable infant in her arms.

I opened my mouth to apologize, but the woman looked at the milk in my hands and immediately started weeping. It was a cry of helpless relief, the kind a drowning person cries after being rescued and brought safely to shore. "We had nothing left to feed the baby," she gasped, "I just prayed for milk...and here you are!"

God could have brought milk to that woman through any variety of means. But I am grateful that He used me. While it took me on a detour and required some courage, the faith that I received in return was well worth the investment. That day continues to inspire me, challenging me to keep listening for His voice, living generously, and being His hands and feet.

CHAPTER EIGHT

Dragonfly

I'm Dodie, and this is my true story.

Dodie

One day as I was driving down the road, I was hit by a drunk driver. The impact forced my head into the driver's side window, shattering the glass. That caused the most serious and lasting injury from the crash: a hole in one of my retinas.

After discussing with the eye surgeon, I learned surgery should be a last resort. I have genetically weak retinas, and the surgeon was unsure if they could hold up to the surgery normally used for this injury. Instead, he said, I should come in weekly for monitoring. Barring surgery, there was no good option. Almost apologetically, the surgeon, who was quite experienced with this issue, offered the best treatment he could: I should try to eliminate stress and get plenty of rest. Week in and week out, I visited him. He tested me over and over, each time with no discernable change.

Meanwhile, I had recently started attending a new church. One Sunday, they were offering something they called "Hands-on Healing." I prayed a brief prayer to God as I walked up: "I'm not sure about this, but I'm going to try it. I trust you." It was simple; I told them about my retina, and they prayed for me for a few minutes. I felt no different.

The following Wednesday, I had my next eye appointment. It started the same as every time before: they injected the dye, and the surgeon carefully reviewed the results in a machine. This time, though, the surgeon was quiet for much longer than usual. Finally, he put one hand on either side of the desk and pushed back his rolling chair, turning to face me. He looked perplexed and astonished. "What did you do in a week? The hole is completely closed!" He had never seen anything like it.

"Do you really want the truth?" I asked.

"Of course, I'm a surgeon!"

"Prayer," I told him. He was silent. He could not believe the truth. Nevertheless, my eye was healed and has remained so to this day.

***

One of the most terrifying moments of my life was when I got the call that my husband, Jim, a construction worker, had fallen two and a half stories and landed headfirst on concrete. He was in a coma for weeks. When he finally became conscious again, it was clear his brain had sustained severe damage. He was in the hospital for months with very little improvement. He could not even speak.

On Valentine's Day, as I was about to visit my husband in the hospital, I received a phone call from my insurance agent. He heard Jim was in an accident. Even though our relationship up to that point had been purely business, my agent asked if there was anything I would like prayer for.

All my life, I had attended church, but mine was a stagnant faith. I went through the motions, but I was not used to praying out loud, certainly not for anything drastic. Nevertheless, as my insurance agent asked, I told him I would love to hear my husband's voice again. The man prayed for me on the phone, a beautiful prayer. It gave me chills. It gave me hope.

When I walked into my husband's hospital room moments later, he smiled at me with his eyes. He slowly opened his mouth and clumsily said, "Happy Valentine's Day. I love you!" He was far from healed; his speech was severely impaired, and his body was still broken. He would need months, maybe years of healing and therapy, but his words on Valentine's Day were like seeing the first ray of sunlight break through the clouds after a storm.

After about six months in the hospital, we were able to bring Jim home. He was under 24-hour care. For the next year and a half, our home was a revolving door of nurses, therapists, and visitors.

Then Jim had a heart attack.

3am at his bedside. Jim lay there in a medically-induced coma. I was physically shaking with fear and anger. After years of Jim's effort, he was just barely able to sit up in his wheelchair on his own. Would all of that work be for nothing? After two years of painstaking recovery, would God let Jim die now?

I cried and trembled as I prayed to God, "I don't want to lose my husband. What are your plans? I need to know. You need to tell me."

At that instant, my husband sat straight up in bed. I stared in disbelief. He opened his mouth and said, clear as day, "God says I have more souls to save." Then he lay back down and remained in a coma until the doctors brought him out of it later.

Jim was released from the hospital shortly afterwards. Then something amazing happened: he starting recovering more quickly than ever from his construction accident two years prior. Although he still spoke with some impairment, people could now understand him. He was even able to get his driver's license.

My husband became a champion of the men's ministry at our church, which met before service on Sundays. Jim would drive himself there and be the first to arrive. He navigated around the building in his electric wheelchair, setting up for the other men. If anyone was late, he would throw donuts at them because he said if he could do it, they had no excuse. My husband even gave speeches at their events. He brought many other men to the Lord.

About two and a half years after his heart attack, my husband was out in our driveway when a garbage truck backed into him, pulling him under the truck and breaking his femur.

That evening, several men from our church asked Jim, "What prayer do you need, brother?"

"I need a new body. Will you pray for a new body?" They did.

The next day, my husband had a lethal heart attack. God answered that prayer by giving Jim a new body in Heaven. No more pain, no more tears. He could run, jump, sing, and dance again. Best of all, Jim got to be with Jesus in paradise.

Although I now see the blessing of God's mercy to take my husband to be with Him, I was devastated at the time. I was left to raise three kids on my own, but my most immediate concern was my husband. I had a restlessness in my soul; had my husband gone to Heaven? Where was he? I prayed, "God, I need to know he's okay. Please show me where he is."

I must have drifted off to sleep as I prayed. I saw a vision. I was in the clouds and saw two figures in front of me, clothed in white. They were embracing. The taller of the two faced me; it was Jesus. The man in His arms was my husband. Even though it was just the back of his head, I recognized him. It was his brown hair, even down to his little bald spot. Jim was in the arms of Jesus. It was so peaceful, so loving. Knowing where my husband was calmed my soul.

The next morning, a good friend of mine unexpectedly came to visit. When I opened the door to greet her, I saw she was holding a package wrapped in brown paper. "I brought you a gift," she said.

As I took the package in my hands, I could feel a picture frame beneath the thin paper. I tore the paper off, and my mouth dropped open. The scene was set in the clouds. Two figures, dressed in white, embraced. The man whose face was visible was Jesus. The other man, with brown hair like my husband's, even had a little bald spot. As I studied the picture, amazed, that same familiar feeling of peace from the night before washed over me. God had sent this picture to confirm the vision I had seen and to keep as a reminder of where my husband would forever be.

Although I had never seen it before, I later learned it was a painting called "The Homecoming."

Some time later, my children and I were watching a movie called *Dragonfly*. In the movie, the protagonist's pregnant wife, who loves dragonflies, tragically dies in an accident. After her death, the main character, Joe, keeps seeing dragonflies behaving unusually. Eventually, his curiosity leads Joe to discover that his daughter survived the accident, at which point he is reunited with her.

The movie got me thinking. My husband and I used to sing together at weddings and such, so we had a few songs that were special to us. Since his death, I would be listening to the radio, and three of our songs would play in a row! I wondered: is he trying to communicate with me? Is God trying to comfort me in my grief?

The day after we watched the movie, I walked out to my front lawn and saw a stunning dragonfly on our tree, just sitting there on the trunk. It was massive and colorful. I was sure it was fake or my children had found it somewhere and placed it on the tree for me. I walked up to it and touched it. It gently moved its wings up and down as I touched its back. As I watched, I knew God had sent this dragonfly to comfort me.

I was a widow for about eight and a half years before I met Kipp. I was hesitant to get into a relationship because of my kids and grandchildren. It was an important decision – many others would be affected. But Kipp was amazing. He was a man of God, joyful and kind. Although he had been heartbroken from his previous marriage, he opened his heart to me and my family. I felt myself falling for him, but I wanted to be sure.

One weekend, we were at Kipp's church, and the pastor was talking about marriage. I could tell Kipp and I were moving in that direction, so I took the opportunity to pray, "God, is this the man I should be with for the rest of my life? I need you to give me a sign."

As Kipp and I were walking out to the parking lot after service, I told him about my prayer. We got to the truck and got in. Kipp rolled his window down, and immediately, a dragonfly flew in and landed on his shoulder.

I had told him my other dragonfly story before, so when the dragonfly landed on him, he was amazed. We both knew it was a sign. We were married soon after. Our marriage has been a beautiful blessing to us all.

My life has been marked by tragedy. Aside from my husband dying, five of my siblings have died premature deaths. *Five.* I have learned I cannot depend on anyone here on Earth. Life is so fragile, so temporary. A sister, a brother, a best friend, a husband may be here one moment and gone the next.

However, I do not fear. I am not anxious about what may come. I know the paradise that awaits me and my brothers and sisters in Christ. The greatest moments on Earth will pale in comparison with Heaven, where the most intoxicating joy we have ever known will be multiplied a hundredfold and stretched into eternity.

While I am waiting to go there, I can depend on only one person: God. He is my hope. I know He loves me and is always with me, no matter what. While my pain on Earth may feel unbearable, it will soon be forgotten when I am reunited with my siblings. I grieve my loss, but I celebrate their gain. And through it all, I hold fast to the promise that God works all things together for the good of those who love Him. I may not understand my hardships and losses yet, but I know my loving Father has a plan and that He is good.

When I am in His arms at last, I imagine He will hold me like I saw Him holding my husband. He will stroke my hair gently, explain to me His glorious plans, and tell me for all eternity how much He loves me.

CHAPTER NINE

Picture Perfect

I'm Robin, and this is my true story.

I was getting increasingly involved with music at my church. I had learned about a week-long intensive for Christian artists – with workshops, nightly concerts, and opportunities to meet with professionals in the industry. It sounded like an amazing opportunity, so I prayed with some friends at church that God would provide a way for me to go. Soon afterward, I got my tax return, and it was the exact amount I needed. I immediately bought my ticket.

A few days later, on a Wednesday morning, I was telling my friend Lisa and her mother about my upcoming trip. Lisa's mother was especially excited and urged me to bring a camera so I could show everyone pictures from my experience. I agreed and told her I would try.

While Lisa and I drove away later that day, I kept thinking about what her mother had said. I did not own a camera, and I felt a growing, inexplicable restlessness about it. The unsettled feeling drove me to stop. I pulled over, smiled awkwardly at Lisa, and asked her if we could take a moment to pray for a camera. She nodded, so I prayed, "God, if it's your will, I would love to have a camera for this trip, but if not, would you please take this restlessness from me? Amen."

I did not normally pray for material things; in fact, I felt silly asking for a camera. It seemed so selfish and trivial. Feeling slightly embarrassed, I laughed as we pulled away from the curb. After about a quarter of a block, we reached an intersection. As the car stopped, so did my heart. I froze for a moment.

I could not take my eyes away from it, even as they began to fill with tears. Without looking away, I put the car in neutral and set the brake. I got out of the car, feeling like I was in slow motion, and ran to the middle of the intersection where I picked up the nicest camera I had ever held.

Any camera would have been a miracle, but this was not just any camera. It was a huge camera with a Minolta telephoto lens, a camera any professional would have been proud to have. I cradled it in both arms and walked back, shaking with excitement and streaming tears. I could see Lisa's face through the windshield. Her mouth was open in happy disbelief. She was crying and shaking her head slowly.

When I got back in the car, we spent several minutes alternating between crying and laughing, sometimes doing both at the same time. Eventually, Lisa confirmed what we both knew: "Robin, this is a miracle!" A few minutes later, she asked, "Does your church still have Wednesday night services?"

"Yes," I said.

"I'd like to go with you," she told me. That night, we went to church together. I later learned that Lisa had been struggling in her faith, but she re-dedicated her life to Jesus that evening. Many others did the same when, at my pastor's request, I shared the camera miracle with my church.

Sometimes, God performs miracles like the parting of the Red Sea: affecting countless multitudes, suspending the laws of physics that He established. Sometimes, though, God's masterminded orchestrations seem to center on just one or two people.

Though my request felt trivial, God wanted me to seek Him even then. Perhaps God cares about the things we think are insignificant because He sees them as opportunities for us to connect with Him and glimpse His majesty. And surely the camera miracle was not the most important thing that happened that day; God leveraged my small request to bring Lisa back to Him. Many people were impacted by the camera story, but Lisa's life through the Holy Spirit has done far more.

The camera was a blessing to me for many years, until one day it mysteriously vanished. When I realized it was gone, I smiled to myself and thought, "Someone else must have prayed for a camera."

CHAPTER TEN

Living Water

I'm Steffani, and this is my true story.

Steffani

While I was growing up in Dodge City, Kansas, I was very involved in church. My closest friends were in youth group, and I had a personal relationship with Jesus. I knew God loved humanity, but I questioned if He loved me as an individual. Once, on my knees as a 13-year-old, I prayed, "Do you see *me*? Do you care for *me*?"

About a month after I prayed that prayer, my parents told me that in two weeks, we would be moving to Colorado, away from everything and everyone I knew. I was devastated. The day after I got the news we would be moving, we went to church. As soon as I arrived, I told all of my friends from youth group.

There was crying and hugging, but most of all, there was a sense of urgency to take full advantage of the time we had left together. We decided to go to a swimming pool that afternoon in a nearby town about 30 minutes away. After we got permission to go and settled some of the logistics, it was time for the service to start, so we went inside the sanctuary.

While the pastor was delivering the sermon, he took a pause and said, "I feel like there is someone here who needs extra prayer for protection." My father felt the Holy Spirit prompting him that he needed that prayer for our family. He raised his hand. My mother assumed he raised his hand because we were moving soon. The church prayed for extra protection for our family, and then we did not think much about it for a few hours.

After church, some of the older kids drove us to the pool. There were about a dozen of us, including my friend Tami. When we arrived, we saw the pool was as packed as we had ever seen it. In fact, we learned that because it was so hot, they had allowed over a hundred extra people into the pool. There were people everywhere, and the water that was visible between them looked murky; we found out later it was because the cleaning system was broken, causing extra chlorine in the water.

Neither of those things stopped us, though. We were determined to enjoy our time there. As Tami and I stood on the edge of the deep end, her cousin, who also happened to be at the crowded pool that day, made a game of pushing us in. Then we would climb back out laughing, and he would do it again.

The lifeguard blew the whistle for a break, and we took the opportunity to have a quick snack. When the whistle sounded again, Tami and I made our way back to the deep end. As we were standing there, her cousin saw his opportunity and decided to resume our game. But we did not know he was coming.

We felt a strong push in our backs. She surged forward, but I was more relaxed – my body absorbed most of the force. It was enough to send me into the water, but not enough to keep my head from striking the edge of the pool on my way in, knocking me unconscious. Tami's cousin had not watched us enter the water. In fact, no one noticed I had hit my head.

I was facedown when my body bobbed back toward the surface. The momentum of the push had been enough to send me drifting forward slowly. When Tami resurfaced, she thought I was just swimming to the other side. As I drifted, I began to sink. The pull of the drain brought me to the bottom of the deep end and held me there.

Tami began to worry. She knew I was fairly shy, especially around strangers. I normally would have stayed by her side. It was certainly uncharacteristic of me to disappear without an explanation. She approached the lifeguard: "I think my friend needs help; could you check in the pool?"

The lifeguard assumed Tami could not find me simply because there were so many people there. "I'm going to ask that you keep looking for her. I'm sure you'll find her! If somebody had needed help, I would have seen it."

Tami was not convinced. She had already thoroughly searched the pool. She approached the older kids from our youth group who were lying on their towels, and she explained the situation to them. They agreed to split up and look for me. They searched everywhere: outside the fence, the concession stand, the restrooms, even on the roof where kids sometimes sunbathed.

The pastor's daughter called my name, "Steffani! Steffani!" When she was met with silence, a feeling washed over her that something was deeply wrong.

The only other place my friends could think to look was the deep end. Two girls began to dive down to see if they could find me. Being unaccustomed to diving, though, they struggled to reach the bottom. Meanwhile, Tami again pleaded with the lifeguard to check in the pool.

A young man overheard. He interjected, "I think I saw someone in the deep end! I know where she is! I grew up in this pool; I can go get her!" Immediately, he dove into the deep end, was able to pop his ears on the way down, and located me on the bottom of the pool – I was wrapped around the drain in the fetal position.

I became aware and saw my body on the bottom of the pool. I saw myself separate from my body, and I walked along the bottom of the pool to the silver steps on the side. I climbed out of the pool and realized I was by myself. There was no one else in sight.

What happened next was indescribable. It was like I was transported, in an instant, through time and space. There were colors and lights far ahead of me. Suddenly, I arrived at the gates of Heaven. I felt cradled safely in God's hands. There was no fear, sorrow, or pain, only a deep peace and contentment. But then I heard a voice I knew was Satan: "She's coming with me!"

***

As my friend Dan helped to lift my body out of the pool, it was clear to him I was gone. My body was completely limp, and there was no life in my eyes, not to mention the fact I had been underwater for thirty minutes or more.

They laid my body next to the edge of the pool. Three hundred mouths turned dead silent. My friend Julie recalls that from the silence emerged the name of Jesus being repeated over and over in quiet whispers.

The lifeguard rushed over and immediately began CPR while Tami ran to the front desk and called my parents. My father answered. Tami said, "They found Steff on the bottom of the pool. She's not breathing. They say she's dead, but you better come now. They're going to take her to the hospital."

The hospital in that small town was half nursing home, half hospital. The ambulance, which was not even equipped with oxygen, came from the mortuary. As the ambulance drove me away, my friend who rode with me petitioned the paramedics. "You have to do something! Shouldn't you at least roll her on her side?" They were not equipped or prepared to deal with a drowning victim. Besides, I was clearly gone. It had been too long, far too long. By the time I was in the ambulance, it had been nearly an hour since I had taken my last breath.

When we arrived at the hospital, we learned that the only doctor on staff was out for the day, and the rest of the staff had little to no experience with drowning victims. When they called the doctor for guidance, he said, "If she's already gone, there's nothing I can do."

Right when my parents got the phone call, a family friend was arriving at their house to practice a song she would perform with my mother at church. As my parents ran out of the house and briefly explained what happened, she decided to stay and pray for me. She walked throughout our house, declaring that I would live. She prayed for my brain, that there would be no permanent damage, and that I would be a miracle.

Many other members of our church were notified and began praying all over our town.

Meanwhile, my parents were racing to meet me. As they drove, my father was reminded of what God had spoken to him during church that day. There must have been a reason God prompted him like that. "My daughter will not die," he prayed out loud as he drove. Pounding the dashboard with tears blurring his vision, "My daughter will live and not die! God, I prayed this morning, and you are faithful. I have covered my family with the blood of Jesus. Steffani will live!"

My mom was praying silently. She told God, "I don't want my daughter to be a vegetable; that is not life. If you can't perform a complete miracle, please take her home. I know that's a miracle, too. If you can do a complete miracle, though, please let my daughter live."

My parents had been to the swimming pool, but they did not know where the hospital was. Nevertheless, they continued at a breakneck pace. Suddenly, a familiar red truck passed them. It was my parents' best friends, the Websters, whom I considered my second parents. They had received a call right after my parents. They took the lead and guided my parents to the hospital.

***

"No, she's not," replied God. Satan continued to demand I come with him. God continued to deny him. Then God ended the altercation definitively: "No, she's not. It's not her time yet, and when it is, she'll be with me." Immediately, I returned to my body.

I found myself in the hospital, where they had wheeled my body out into a hallway and covered it with a sheet. The hospital staff had nothing left they could do. My body would stay there until my parents could see it, after which it would be transported to the morgue.

I became aware of my friends gathered around me, whispering and sobbing. A figure ran down the hall towards me – it was my father. I cannot imagine the weight of his pain as he pulled back the sheet to see his daughter. Or the depth of relief when I opened my eyes and met his. "Hi, Daddy," I said.

It hurt to breathe and it hurt to speak, but I was able to say enough to the nurses that they could tell I did not have the severe brain damage they would have expected from someone who had gone without oxygen for so long. Not knowing what to do with me, they sent me home.

Meanwhile, my friends and family were celebrating, praising, shouting, laughing. They called everyone who had been praying to tell them what had happened. When I arrived home, our house was a constant flow of our church friends. I felt groggy and overwhelmed. Eventually, I lost consciousness.

Unsure what to do, my parents called the Dodge City hospital. "Bring her right in," they said. When I arrived at the emergency room, the doctor flooded my parents with questions as I went in and out of consciousness. My parents did their best to answer with what my friends had told them, but I felt the need to speak. Finally, I was able to take a deep breath and say, "I know the answer. Jesus saved me today; he saved my life!"

The doctor clapped her hands together and said, "It's a miracle, it's a miracle!"

As the doctor inspected me, she touched my head, and I winced with pain. She pulled back my hair to discover where I had hit my head on the edge of the pool. She diagnosed me with a concussion, the reason for my grogginess. I had also swallowed some of the overly chlorinated water, which caused my throat to burn. However, the doctor was astonished to find I had no water in my lungs.

They wanted to keep me overnight to monitor me. During my entire stay at the hospital, my room was a hive of doctors and nurses who had heard about my miracle and wanted to see the girl God saved. Already, He was being glorified through this miracle.

Later, as I was reflecting on everything that had happened, I compared my experience to other stories I had heard. When others left their bodies, they saw everyone around them, but I had seen no one. It was only me. I prayed for clarity. "God, why didn't I see anyone else?" For a long time, I did not receive a clear answer.

Months went by, and the chaos faded into excitement. The excitement faded into contentment. I continued to ask God that question: "Why was it only me?" Finally, I received my answer:

"Steff, didn't you ask me if I loved *you*? If I saw *you*? I wanted you to see that day through my eyes. I saw only you. I always see you, and I always love you just the way you are. I am the One who breathed life into you, my precious daughter. Because of that, I want you to go and tell others I see *them*, and I love *them*, and I can do miracles for them as well."

CHAPTER ELEVEN

Aggressive Treatment

I'm Ralph, and this is my true story.

Ralph

On October of 2008, I visited my doctor for my regular physical. Due to my age, my check-ups include a test for prostate-specific antigen (PSA). Higher levels of the antigen indicate a possibility of prostate cancer.

Everything looked good during my physical, but we had to wait for the results on the bloodwork and PSA. Once the results were in, my doctor called me and said she would like to speak with me about the test.

When I arrived, she reassured me that all of my levels looked well within acceptable limits. However, she noticed a small anomaly in my PSA results. She was almost apologetic, explaining she did not know why it was bothering her; she knew of no cause for concern. All of her knowledge and experience on the subject indicated my PSA results were as they should be. However, she said she would like me to visit the urologist just in case.

The next available appointment for the urologist was about a month later. He also conducted a PSA test, and the results were fine again. Nevertheless, the urologist decided to take biopsy samples of my prostate.

A few days later, when the results came in, the urologist asked me to come in to discuss the biopsy. I sat down, and the urologist sighed. He looked me in the eyes and told me, "You have stage four prostate cancer."

I could not say anything. His words echoed in my head. They were for someone else, as though I had just watched someone in a movie receive a diagnosis. Not me. I looked at the cold, tiled floor.

Then, I heard a gentle voice in my mind – I knew it was God: *Be at peace about this.* That comforted me. Even though it was some of the most life-altering news I had ever received, I felt a profound sense of calm because I was reminded God is greater than all of it, and He can bring me out of any danger. I will not be on this Earth a moment more or less than He intends, so why should I worry?

Driving home, I realized I needed that peace not only for myself, but also for my family. They needed to see the transcendent calm I felt. When I told them the news later, they were understandably shaken. However, my assurance comforted my family, especially my wife.

After discussing treatment options with the doctor, we decided to remove the prostate using robotics, the most reliable option. The surgery went well. In fact, I felt hardly any pain afterward.

The next day, when the nurses learned how well my recovery was progressing, they asked me how I felt about taking a walk. I agreed to, and we walked around the hallway for a while. I felt great the whole time. When I made it back to my room, my doctor and nurse were waiting for me, checking on my progress. I sat down in a chair.

I suddenly awoke. The room was full of medical staff. I asked them what was happening, and they told me my heart had stopped, and they had resuscitated me. Thankfully, my wife had not been in the room at the time, so she did not have to witness the traumatic event. The even greater blessing, though, was that my heart had stopped as medical staff were in the room, so they had acted quickly. If this had happened with no one else present, it could have been much, much worse. Had my heart stopped at home, I likely would have died. All the men in my family have suffered from heart issues, but I had none before this. Thankfully, God waited until I was in the safest place possible to allow my heart issues to show themselves.

Before I left the hospital from my cancer surgery, I received a pacemaker as well. The doctors also took another biopsy of my prostate to see if there was any cancer remaining.

Shortly afterward, we received news there was still some cancer in the margins, but they would not treat it at this time, only monitor it with PSA tests. I told the doctors that was fine; I would simply pray the cancer would never return.

For three years afterward, I had no treatment whatsoever. The doctors continued to test me and monitor my progress, but everything was fine. Until the third year, when the tests revealed a sudden resurgence of the cancer. When the doctors confirmed the cancer had returned, they recommended an "aggressive treatment plan."

"No," I said. "My aggressive treatment is going to be the Lord. I am going to take three months and seek prayer, then you can run the tests again."

I had never sought prayer for healing before, but I had faith God would heal me. I found a prayer ministry at my church and began to attend regularly. Weekly, I returned to ask for prayer. Two weeks. I felt no different. Four weeks. I persevered. Eight weeks.

On Thursday night of the eighth week, I had a dream. A pastor from my church was there, dressed in a black suit. He addressed a room full of people with a somber tone. All of my loved ones were listening from their seats. In the middle of the room just in front of the stage was a casket. It was my funeral.

When I awoke, I was deeply troubled. Nevertheless, I went back on Saturday to receive prayer. Before we started praying, I told the man who was praying for me about my dream. "Oh," he began with a comforting smile, "don't be concerned. That funeral was not for you. It was for your cancer."

I instantly felt a peace in my heart and a confidence I would be cancer free. Still, I waited until the end of the twelve weeks as I had promised the doctors. We ran the tests again. To the doctors' amazement, I was cancer free. Even several years later, it has not returned.

I give all the glory to God, but I am also incredibly thankful to all of the doctors involved, especially my physician who recommended I see a urologist even though she had no basis for concern. I believe she was responding to a prompting from the Holy Spirit which saved my life.

Through this journey, God had been building my faith – from the peace He spoke in a dark moment to saving my heart in the hospital. He has always been faithful, so when the cancer returned, I felt confident laying it at His feet. Earth-shaking fears melt in the loving hands of the Architect; considering His cosmic power and limitless love, how could I be afraid?

CHAPTER TWELVE

Unconscious

I'm Duane, and this is my true story.

I felt well-rested when I woke up that morning. I started the day with my usual nutrition shake and workout. Then I headed to church where I was leading worship, one of the best parts of my life for the past 14 years or so.

As we began the worship set, things were going well, but after a song or two, I started feeling strange. I thought maybe if I closed my eyes for a moment, the feeling would pass. I suddenly found myself on the floor, and people were rushing toward me to carry me backstage.

As I regained consciousness, I tried to figure out what had happened. Without any other apparent culprit, the only cause I could imagine was low blood sugar, so I drank a sports drink. I felt fine afterward and even went back out for the final worship song at the end of the service.

In the months following, I never had any other symptoms. There was a lingering apprehension that I had some undiagnosed medical problem or that it would happen again, but it never did. On Christmas Eve, I learned why.

I was leading worship again on Christmas Eve, some six months after I went unconscious onstage. After the service, a young man approached me and asked if he could speak with me for a moment.

Stepping aside, he told me about a dark time in his life approximately six months prior. He had been questioning his faith and was angry at God. Although he did not want to be in church that day, his family had pressured him to come. He stood in the worship service ready to renounce his faith entirely. But one last time, he had prayed, "God, if you're real, make that man fall down."

"I guess I need to apologize," he told me, "because I prayed that prayer about you." My heart swelled from appreciation and amazement. How incredible for God to use me in reaching out to a wayward son. What a bold gesture God had made.

In my astonishment, I was temporarily speechless and could only laugh, shaking my head in wonder. I eventually thanked him for telling me. I felt great relief knowing the reason I fell was not some mysterious medical condition. "However," I joked with him, "Next time you need a target, you could pray for God to put a million dollars in my pocket!"

The young man laughed and proceeded to tell me how God had changed his life since. His faith is now unassailable. He even enrolled in seminary to become a pastor and share Jesus with others.

Who knows why that young man was angry with God? Perhaps it seemed God had not heard him about a crucial prayer. Or maybe God seemed absent during a time of great need. I cannot say why He may have appeared to be silent or absent. However, I can testify that God loves that man enough to make me swoon.

(In almost two years since, I have had no other fainting episodes or any related issues.)

CHAPTER THIRTEEN

Sufficient

I'm Sarah, and this is my true story.

About six and a half years ago, I was expecting our third child. As my husband Ben and I prepared for our new arrival, we discussed the possibility of Ben seeking a new job. It would make things easier if he earned a higher salary, and Ben was excited at the prospect of a new adventure.

After plenty of prayer and careful consideration, we felt like God had told us yes, Ben could look for a new job. He looked casually for a couple of months and found few that seemed like a good fit. There was, however, one position he was excited about.

Ben carefully prepared his resume. He was well-qualified and confident. All throughout the application process, we prayed for Ben to get this job. Then came the interview.

He was ready, well-dressed and well-rehearsed. We said a prayer before he left. As I watched Ben walk out of the front door, I felt a swell of pride and a strong sense of hope that God was preparing us for a new season of blessing and adventure.

Ben called me after his interview. His tone was optimistic. As we talked through how it went, both he and I felt he had done his best, and we were confident that at any moment, he would receive a phone call offering him the position. But the call did not come. After a couple of days, we learned the position had gone to someone else.

Frankly, we were angry with God. Why had He told us to seek a new job only to have our hopes dashed? Why would He let us get so far in the process only to fall short of the prize?

Sometimes, when God's answer is *no*, we never learn *why* until we get to Heaven. Sometimes, we get the blessing of learning *why* on this side of eternity. We did not fully realize our *why* until nearly six months later.

Our third child arrived soon afterward, so we were too busy to think about finding a new job. Once while I was awake in the middle of the night with my new baby, I noticed Ben was having difficulty breathing. After discussing it with him, we decided to have him do a sleep study to see if he had sleep apnea.

After he finished the sleep study, Ben was supposed to check in with his doctor to go over the results. When he went in for the appointment, Ben was sitting with the doctor while an assistant went to retrieve the file on his sleep study. The file was nowhere to be found. They insisted it had been sitting on the doctor's desk just before Ben had come in, but now it had inexplicably disappeared.

Ben had planned on a quick in-and-out visit. However, since they had to wait to locate the missing file, Ben decided to mention something to the doctor that he would have otherwise kept to himself.

His whole life, my husband has been very healthy. He gets sick less often than other people and recovers more quickly. Perhaps because of this, he rarely visits doctors, opting instead to wait and see if ailments will disappear on their own. On that particular day, Ben had some discomfort in his side. He assumed he had pulled a muscle or something while fighting the flu the week before. Certainly, though, it was minor enough he would not have given it a second thought had he not been sitting in awkward silence next to an unoccupied doctor.

When Ben mentioned the discomfort, the doctor was curious and decided to investigate. As he prodded Ben's side, he noticed something concerning. While a normal man's spleen is not externally palpable, Ben's spleen was easily palpable, enlarged several times its normal size.

The doctor immediately ordered Ben to undergo a battery of tests. The next four days was a blur – visiting office after office, specialist after specialist. That in itself was a minor miracle; most of those places had waiting lists several weeks long. However, we believe God orchestrated it so we could get in exactly when we needed to. Someone would mysteriously cancel their appointment. There would be a scheduling error in our favor. The doctor would make an exception and stay late just for Ben.

At the end of the five days, we finally received the diagnosis.

Leukemia.

Ben's form of leukemia was incredibly aggressive. It was only one week from when Ben mentioned the discomfort in his side to when he began chemotherapy, but by the time he began treatment, he could barely stand. Tragically, most people with his diagnosis are mere days from death when they are finally diagnosed.

However, because of the mysteriously missing sleep study results, Ben mentioned an otherwise innocuous discomfort to his doctor, leading to an uncommonly early diagnosis. The doctors later said he had probably only had leukemia for two weeks by the time he was diagnosed. As a result, Ben was much stronger and healthier than most when he began his difficult treatment.

The years that followed have been incredibly challenging. The onslaught of medications, chemotherapy, and complications have almost claimed my husband's life several times. However, we believe God used Ben's early diagnosis to prepare him for that treacherous road and give him the strength he needed to survive.

We also have the blessing of knowing why God said no to the job Ben wanted. If Ben had gotten the job we had been praying so earnestly for, he would have been employed for less than ninety days when he was diagnosed. That company would have had no reason to keep him employed.

Throughout this illness, there have been long stretches when Ben is completely unable to work. Right after his diagnosis was one of them. If Ben had gotten that new job, they would have had no requirement to keep him employed or insured. We would have lost our insurance coverage, and Ben's expensive treatments would have landed us in bankruptcy within the first two months of his illness. We would have lost *everything*.

However, because God said *no*, Ben stayed at his company. When Ben's company learned of his diagnosis, they told us they did not want us to worry about anything except Ben getting better. Not only that, but they sent out an email to the entire company explaining that Ben would be unable to work for at least six months. They invited employees to donate vacation time to support our family, and the response was overwhelming. The vacation time we received amounted to almost a full year's wages.

They kept Ben insured as long as they were legally allowed to, and even when they were required to switch Ben to COBRA insurance, they paid for our insurance premiums. They have been incredibly generous, far above and beyond what any company is expected or required to do. Perhaps most astonishing, the owners of the company have personally come to visit Ben and prayed with him several times.

What we needed was not another job. What we needed was more gratitude for the job Ben already had. What better way than to allow Ben to explore other options and then show us why God had him where he was.

We still do not know exactly why God has allowed Ben to get sick. These six years have been incomparably difficult. They have drastically shifted our perspectives and priorities. They have shaken us to our very core. What we do know is God has used this season to reveal Himself, to us and to others. Many of our family and friends have seen God's tender mercies and miracles through our struggle. While we would not choose this path, we know it is a temporary difficulty. God has given us joy and peace that transcend understanding. Despite overwhelming trials, His grace has always been sufficient for us. We know no matter what, He loves us. And no matter what, this temporal suffering will pale in comparison with an eternity in paradise.

Special thanks to Ben's company, General Air Service and Supply, for all their love and support.

CHAPTER FOURTEEN

On a Wing and a Prayer

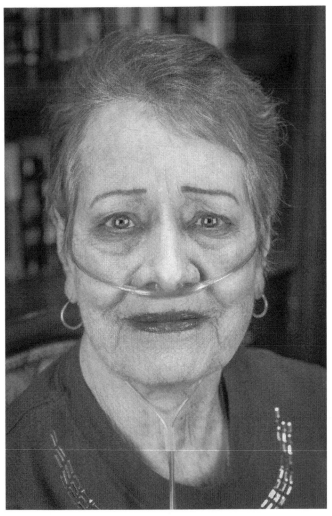

I'm Donna, and this is my true story.

Donna

When my children were young, I used to warn them, "Don't walk by the prison; the people in there are dangerous!"

Then when I was praying one day, I felt God prompting me to do something that made my veins run cold. It could not be. That must not be what God wanted me to do. I continued praying, and the prompting intensified. *Those men are my children. They need to meet me, Donna, and I want you to make the introduction.* I felt terrified and unqualified. I received no further instruction – only an inescapable prompting that God wanted me to reach out to those "dangerous" men. God gave me the destination, but He did not provide the action plan.

With no idea where to begin, I simply went to the prison and asked questions. When I inquired about starting a ministry, the board of directors said I needed to apply and write a letter explaining why they should allow my ministry into the prison.

I had no idea what to write, so I prayed about it. I felt God tell me, *Write, "Because I said so."* So I did.

When I submitted my application, I held out a page and said, "Here is my letter of explanation." It was a full page, blank except one line that simply said, "Because God said so."

I later learned from a board member that their deciding meeting was heated. One board member, who had served on the board for over a decade, maintained strong objections. He worried we would bring music into the prison and have worship services, an accurate assumption. He told the rest of the board that if they let me in, he would resign immediately.

It eventually came to a vote. Every single member of the board voted to allow my prison ministry. Except one member, who walked out immediately, never to return.

As I built the prison ministry, God blessed it immensely. He was using it to transform the lives of the inmates involved and help them to escape a system that had formerly claimed them – past, present, and future. In fact, about 97% of the inmates involved in our ministry were not returning to prison when they were released, instead becoming productive, respected members of society. God was softening many hard hearts, many whose walls seemed as impregnable as the prison walls.

There were other walls coming down though, another heart softening: my own. I began to realize that the inmates were not the only beneficiaries of this ministry. God had called me not because I was the most effective person to lead this ministry, but because He wanted to teach me about the reach of His love. There is no one too broken, too lost, too dangerous for Him. He loves them all, and He wants His people to share that message with everyone who will hear.

I used my newfound conviction to fuel my passion and redouble my efforts to reach the lost people in the prisons. But it was not enough for me. Even with all of our encouraging results, I felt a discomfort, a growing tension between the time I had to spend at my job and the time I wanted to invest in the prison ministry. I wished I could do more. Then suddenly, I lost my job.

I had two sons at home, and I was raising them by myself. Things had already been financially difficult, but having no job made survival seem impossible. But God specializes in the impossible.

As I prayed one day about what to do, I felt God speaking to me, *You know that tension you've been feeling between your work and mine? It's gone. Now you have more time to be in the prison!* Despite my natural, logical inclination to seek other employment, I felt God leading me to volunteer in the prison full time.

I considered how God provided manna in the wilderness every day for 40 years. I remembered how the disciples lived during their ministry, saving nothing, taking nothing with them, God providing their every need, just in time. I recalled the Lord's Prayer, "Give us this day our daily bread." I decided to trust Him for provision.

One of the enduring truths from that season is this: if God called me to a season of need, He would meet those needs. The following years were difficult in many ways, but I saw God everywhere. There were so many miracles that it is difficult to remember them all, but here are a few that I will never forget:

With virtually no income, we would soon face homelessness, a problem I had been praying about frequently. Without me telling her about my concerns, one of my friends approached our pastor. "We give so much to foreign ministries; can we give to one right here in our hometown?" She then explained my prison ministry and gave him my phone number.

When the pastor called, he asked me one question, "How can we help you?"

I answered honestly, "My sons and I need a home."

Then he made an offer that changed our lives forever. "I want you to pick out any trailer, and the church will buy it for you."

That trailer has been an incredible blessing to our family and allowed me to continue my prison ministry for many years following. In earthly terms, it was the grandest gesture of God's provision, but there were many more examples that touched my heart as well.

I shared one of my favorites with my granddaughter as we were spending time together one day. We were hungry, but we were all out of food and had no money to buy any. "What will we do, Grandma?" she asked.

"Pray," I replied. And we did. The next time we opened the front door, there were three bags full of groceries sitting on our porch.

My granddaughter did not grasp the improbability of it – she simply squealed with delight, trotted over to the bags, and began unloading them. She missed the magnitude. It was as though she had asked her father for a cookie and he had simply given it to her. She was content, so she happily went on with her life.

As I reflected on the incident later, I realized that perhaps my granddaughter's perspective was correct. Maybe her childlike faith contained all I needed to know. I had longed to give my treasured little one something to eat, and I believe God felt the same way toward us. After all, the Bible says He loves to give His children good gifts. While I did not have the means to provide what we needed, God did.

We asked our Father for something, and He gave it to us. I resolved to be more faithful about asking for what I needed. Just as I wanted to know about and meet my family needs, my Father in Heaven must feel that way about me.

What grieves a Father's heart like a sick child? During my time in prison ministry, I contracted bronchitis and needed medicine, but I had no money, and I did not believe in using credit cards. I had resolved to wait.

One night as I was driving home, I was praying about the situation, asking for God's help, when I felt God tell me, *Go to the supermarket.*

But, God, I prayed, *I don't have any money.* As if he didn't know. Nevertheless, the prompting persisted. I worried I would seem foolish, asking for medicine I could not pay for.

The supermarket was directly on my route home, but I still planned to wait. As I neared the store, though, the prompting got stronger and more insistent, *Donna, go to the supermarket!*

I relented. When I got inside, I went straight to the pharmacy and asked the lady at the counter how long it would take to fill my prescription, neglecting to mention I could not pay for it. "About twenty minutes," she said. I thanked her and walked around the store while I waited.

Exactly twenty minutes later, I returned to the counter and asked for my prescription. As the woman reached for it, I began to ask how much it would cost, "How mu—"

"Donna?" a voice interrupted me. A man wearing a white pharmacist's jacket had just entered next to the woman helping me. He continued, "You don't know me, but I go to your church, and I heard you talk about what you are doing with your prison ministry!" He turned to the woman helping me, "How much is her prescription?"

"$9.99," she responded.

"I'll take care of it," he said. "Go ahead and give it to her."

God used people to give me many gifts, like the trailer and the medicine, but there were some that were undeniably Him. One of those was when God gave me a present for His birthday. One Christmas season, my granddaughter wanted a black bean bag chair for Christmas. I had looked everywhere, but that was one of the popular gifts that year, so everyone was out of stock. As I was thinking about this, I felt the Lord speak to me, *Call the toy store.*

But I already talked to them there, I prayed. *They said they don't have any.*

Call the toy store, the Lord persisted. *They have a surplus container behind the store. They have a bean bag chair inside that container.*

A man answered the phone, "Hi, this is Matt! How can I help you today?" I explained what I was looking for. "I'm sorry, but we don't have any left," he said.

"I think you do," I replied calmly. "Would you please check in the surplus container you have out back behind the store?"

"How do you know about that?" he asked.

"The Lord told me."

A brief pause. "Okay, I will go check." I waited for several minutes. I heard him pick up the receiver, breathing heavily. He was either excited or out of breath, maybe both. "Guess what!" he began hurriedly. "You were right! We had one left, exactly the one you wanted!"

Many years after the bean bag miracle, I moved to a retirement home and left the miracle trailer to my son and his family. Although I still miss going into the prisons, I am encouraged knowing the ministry continues. I now serve on the board of directors; sometimes we even have board meetings here at the retirement home.

God has also given me a new calling. I was praying one day that He would let me go back to the prisons, and I felt Him reply, *Donna, you are surrounded by people who are living in their own personal prisons.*

My life's work now is to bring the light of Jesus to the people all around me at the retirement home who are living in darkness, loneliness, and despair. I have no idea how much longer I will be on this Earth, but I will continue doing this work as long as I am here.

God, too, continues to do His work in my life through His constant goodness and continued miracles. I recently had a health scare that led me to believe I would go to Heaven sooner than I expected. One night when a nurse came in to check on me, she was unable to wake me. They took me to the hospital and found I was experiencing catastrophic organ failure. They called all of my family in and told them I probably would not survive the night. They told them that my kidneys had shut down completely, and many other organs were shutting down as well.

As I lay in the hospital bed fighting to remain conscious, my son leaned down and whispered in my ear, "Mom, what do you want to do? Do you want to live, or do you want to die?"

I looked at him, then up to the ceiling. "I want to do whatever the Lord wants me to do."

The doctors needed to perform surgery to assess the damage on my organs and attempt to slow their shutdown. I prayed before the surgery, "God, please guide the doctors' hands. Show them your light, and tell them what to do."

The surgery began. Suddenly, I could see inside of my stomach. I saw hands moving around, a bright light guiding them. Then I heard someone exclaim, "Wow! Her kidneys are working again! And her other organs are following suit!"

"This is a miracle!" another voice added.

And so I survive today, a living testimony of God's goodness and His miracles. With increasing difficulty but increasing joy, I spend my days testifying to all He has done for me and helping others to find Him. I have forsaken almost everything the world holds dear to pursue Jesus, and I have never regretted it.

Living for anything else is like performing CPR on a dummy. It is exhausting, and there is no life there. Living for God, though, is a fulfilling adventure. It is thrilling and yet somehow peaceful. And every night when I have spent a day doing His work, I fall into bed with a grateful fatigue, the kind that only comes from a long day of rewarding labor. I lie there smiling, anticipating when the One I adore will hold me and tell me, "Well done."

To hear more about Donna's story, other miracles in her life, and the way her prison ministry has saved countless others, read *On a Wing and a Prayer* by Becky Lyles.

CHAPTER FIFTEEN

Home

I'm Karen, and this is my true story.

Karen

My daughter Dawn has always been obsessed with aviation and space, so the birthday gift her husband Shaun gave her was perfect: a gift certificate to go indoor skydiving, something she had never tried before. She absolutely loved it. That spark ignited a passion that would grow far beyond what any of us would have predicted.

Soon, Dawn was no longer simulating skydiving in an indoor facility – she was actually jumping out of airplanes. She told us that as she was plummeting to earth, she imagined this to be what Heaven looks like. She danced on the clouds as the sunlight embraced her. Completely unencumbered, she surrendered to God's presence there in the sky.

Before long, Dawn and some friends had formed a team and started entering competitions, much to the chagrin of my family and me. Although we worried about her well-being, Dawn's safety officer assured us she was his most cautious skydiver. She was also fiercely competitive and gifted at her new sport, winning several awards, both team and individual.

On October 3rd, 2017, Dawn and her team were in Portugal practicing when I received an unexpected call from Shaun's mother. "Karen, I have some bad news. Dawn had a fall. Something went wrong while she was skydiving, and she smashed into the rocks."

I could tell from our conversation that the fall had been devastating, but the extent of Dawn's injuries did not become fully clear until a couple of days afterward, when Shaun was finally able to fly from their home in England to where Dawn had been hospitalized in Portugal. Communicating by phone was cost-prohibitive, but he kept us updated by email. He told us the reason for her fall was unclear, but she had made a low turn causing her to suddenly lose altitude. She had missed her landing site and landed in a rocky area instead. The safety officer told Shaun that Dawn would not have done so without cause, but there was no way to know what the reason was. Equipment failure did not seem to be a factor.

She had hit the rocks, smashed her face, bounced off, and then hit the back of her head on more rocks. In the process, her nose had been pushed inside her head, and her face had shattered. Her skull had fragmented, sending shards of bone into her brain, which was now bathed in blood and under lethal pressure. The rest of her body was a cacophony of broken bones and torn tissues. She lay in an induced coma, her brain activity a barely detectable shudder.

I felt helpless. A world away in Colorado, I did the only thing I felt I could: pray. Not only that, but I recruited everyone possible. My husband told people at work, and they sent the news through their prayer networks. My mother activated her prayer chains in Phoenix. Old friends in Malaysia sent prayers rippling through their circles. Prayers for Dawn encircled the globe.

On Sunday, a few days after receiving the news, I went to church. After the service, they always invite people to come down to the front of the sanctuary if they need prayer, so I did. I told the young man who greeted me there about Dawn's accident, and I showed him a picture of her. As we prayed together, I kept repeating, through barely contained sobs, "Your will be done, your will be done, your will be done…" And then I added, "If you need her, you can have her, but she has a family that really needs her, too. She has children who need her, too."

For the next two weeks, Shaun's updates were a roller coaster. One day, Shaun's emails would seem

131

hopeful, rays of light breaking through the clouds. The next day, there would be a complication, a setback, hopelessness. Part of the reason for this was a language barrier between the doctors and Shaun. Hardly any of the hospital employees spoke English, and when they did, there were often translation errors, especially with medical terminology.

Shaun was not allowed to stay at the hospital, but he found a hotel five minutes away from it. He was with Dawn every moment he could be. He sat with her, stroked her hand, and talked to her about their favorite memories. He believed she could hear him, even if it was somewhere deep in her subconscious, and that his interaction with her could help bring her back to us.

On October 17th, the head doctor had a meeting with Shaun. She had been watching him and his behavior with Dawn. "I feel we may have given you the wrong impression," she said. She showed him Dawn's CT scans since the beginning of her hospitalization and then compared them with a normal brain. She explained to Shaun that Dawn's brain activity had shown no improvement. In fact, she said, Dawn was not clinically brain dead by only the tiniest margin. "Dawn is no longer here," she told him. "Only her body remains. We don't know when her body will be gone – it could be a day, it could be a month," but her firm prognosis was Dawn would not survive. When Shaun pressed her to ask if there was any chance, she responded the chance was very small. If she did survive, the head doctor said, Dawn would certainly need to be hospitalized for the rest of her life. Her brain function had simply been too impaired for too long.

"Go home," she told Shaun. "Your children need you."

***

I told my husband Jerry that I needed to go say goodbye to my daughter.

He found me a flight that had suddenly dropped in price to half of what all of the other flights had cost since Dawn's accident. As I prepared to leave, my supervisor at work asked me for a brief update. By now, everyone had heard about the accident, but rumors had inadvertently developed. I put together a little flier with pictures of Dawn with me; Dawn and Shaun; their kids; and Dawn with her whole skydiving group. This was all I had the heart to write on the flier:

> *My beautiful daughter Dawn is brain-dead,*
> *but her heart is still beating because they*
> *have kept her in a medically-induced coma.*
> *Because she did not have an "official living*
> *will," the hospital can't let us pull the plug.*

Please pray with us that God will stop her
heart and take her HOME.

In many ways, this was my worst nightmare, not only in the general sense that my daughter was gone – Dawn and I had had several conversations before her accident about this scenario. Both of us feared an existence with no quality of life, sustained only by machines. We had made each other promise if we ever found ourselves in that situation, we would pull the plug for the other. Now I found myself helpless to fulfill my tragic promise to my daughter.

October 27th, only ten days after the head doctor had told Shaun to go home, I boarded the plane to say goodbye to my Dawn. As I crossed the ocean, I thought of all those who still clung to a shred of hope, despite all evidence to the contrary. Even Shaun, in his last email, had written this:

> *In my own private corner I don't dare tell*
> *the kids about, I'm clinging to a tiny scrap*
> *of hope. There isn't any. I know. And that*
> *hope is only a faint wisp of a dream.*

Many friends, in their ignorance, still prayed for a miracle. As for me, I could not let myself hope. I had no reason to, and it was too painful anyway. The gavel had landed, the sentence given. I told myself it was over. The only thing left to close the chapter was to say goodbye.

Linda, a skydiving friend of Dawn's, picked me up from the airport and took me to the hotel, the same hotel Shaun had left only days before. Linda also graciously agreed to go with me to the hospital to translate.

When we arrived at the hospital, I was anxious to see my daughter for the first time in months, but the doctors asked to talk with me first. I choked up. The only reason I could imagine they would want to speak with me was that Dawn had already passed away. *At least I'll still be able to give her a hug and kiss,* I thought.

"I don't know where to begin," the doctor said. "We have no explanation for this, but there has been a change in your daughter's condition."

I held my breath.

"The pressure in her brain has gone down, and the blood is gone. She is breathing on her own, but we are still keeping her on the ventilator just in case. She has been moving her eyes behind her eyelids. Her coma has been improving as well, and she is now only on a low dosage of the medication keeping her in a coma. She still has some pneumonia, but that is also improving."

I could not speak for a moment. I stared at Linda in disbelief. I looked at the doctor, who was smiling. "What are you saying? What is he saying?" I stammered.

"Are you sure?" Linda asked him. He was.

I was still in a daze when I walked into Dawn's room. I did not know how to process what I had just heard. Then I saw her. She was unrecognizable except for a mess of blonde hair emerging from a network of tubes and wires. I had to catch my breath for a moment after the initial shock of seeing the reality of my precious daughter's condition. Although her face had been reconstructed and her bones set, her body still bore the evidence of her tragic accident. Stitching, scarring, bruising, swelling – my heart ached to see how my little girl had been wracked.

I walked over to her and took her hand. I gently stroked her forehead and kissed her cheek. "Hi, Honey. Mommy's here." And for the first time since October 3rd, she opened her eyes and looked right at me!

Involuntarily, I stood up and clapped my hands together. "Dawn, can you see me? Dawn, Mommy's here!" The nurses noticed my reaction and hurried over. The next moments were a blur of astonished doctors and nurses checking monitors and making adjustments. As I was jostled about, they encouraged me to keep talking to her, so I did. She opened her eyes several more times and often looked at me as I explained to her what had happened.

When I came out to meet Linda, she was flabbergasted at the news. We spent several minutes in the hospital hallway, jumping with joy, crying and laughing. Linda said, "Karen, we have just witnessed a true miracle."

"I have to call Shaun," I said. "I don't care what it costs. He needs to know!" When I told him, he was silent at first, as though the news could not penetrate. Slowly, he softened, asking a few questions. After several minutes, Shaun was able to allow his tiny scrap of hope to feast on the truth. God had given us a miracle. He had heard our cries and answered us – by giving me back my daughter, Shaun back his wife, the children back their mother.

Every day from then on was an improvement. Soon, Dawn was transferred to a hospital in England near her home. Not long after, she was released from the hospital to a rehabilitation facility. There, she relearned how to speak, how to walk. Having a conversation with her now, it is easy to forget she ever had an accident. She still has trouble with stairs, but she is getting better all the time.

Today, as I write this on August 4th, 2018, I praise God for the fact that Dawn will be transferred next week to her last rehabilitation facility where she will finalize her recovery to become a fully independent and capable mother. It has been a long, hard road, not only for Dawn, but for Shaun, all of our family, and Dawn's many friends. Prayers of thanksgiving and healing are still going around the world.

As I have told Dawn, God must not have wanted her in Heaven yet because He has something special for her down here. Whatever the reason for the miracle, I cannot express the extent of my gratitude. I will be eternally grateful for the thousands of people around the world who prayed for us, for the friends and family who supported and helped us, for the medical professionals whose hands were guided by God to facilitate this recovery. And most importantly, for God's unfailing love.

Even when all hope seems lost, He loves us still. Even when the gavel has fallen and the sentence is pronounced, He loves us still. Even when the chapter seems to have closed, His love continues. Even when the tomb is sealed, His love is stronger than the power of death. And whether He had chosen to save Dawn or not, I am most grateful she and I get to spend eternity with our loving God along with everyone who believes.

CHAPTER SIXTEEN

The Greatest Blessing

I'm Ashley, and this is my true story.

I had a traumatic pregnancy. At first, I thought I was overreacting. I had no point of reference since it was my first child, but there were times when I could not even walk up the stairs because I had no energy. When my daughter was born, though, the problems continued. More than I care to admit, my daughter's first six months were spent in a pack and play next to me while I was on the couch with no strength to lift her out and hold her. Sometimes, my husband even had to bathe me because I could not do it myself.

As I was going through this, I had some family members who were diagnosed with Lyme disease. Knowing my symptoms, they recommended I be tested. The tests revealed I had not only Lyme disease, but also several other co-infections and intestinal parasites. The doctor prescribed a regimen of medicines and treatments to systematically address all of the issues, but he warned me the process would be brutal, and there was a good chance I would feel worse before I felt better.

The doctor was right. I began taking the prescribed medications and progressively felt worse. To have suffered from this disease for over a year only to decline was disheartening. Even though the doctor had warned me, the fact remained this was the worst I had ever felt in my life. I felt like I was losing myself. My personality, my life, atrophying in my disease. I felt hopeless.

I cried out to God in my despair. "I can't do this. I need you to help me." As I was praying, I felt Him clearly tell me, *I want you to stop. Stop, and know me as your Healer.* Instantly, I felt a boldness about what I was going to do.

When I told my husband and my family that I planned to stop the prescribed treatments, they understandably questioned my decision. "If the medicine is supposed to help, why would God tell you to stop taking it?" "How do you know God doesn't want to make you well through what the doctor is doing?" "Are you sure that was God telling you that?" But God had given me a confidence about this decision, and I stood firm.

I stopped taking my medication. Instead, I sought Jesus. I ravenously read the Bible and spent every moment I could in prayer. I studied the Holy Spirit and learned to hear His voice better and better. In my suffering and my weakness, I leaned into God with every last shred of strength.

I used to wonder what it would look like to "Love the Lord [my] God with all [my] heart and with all [my] soul and with all [my] strength and with all [my] mind" (Luke 10:27). If I was honest with myself, before I stopped taking my medication, I did not know what that meant. I did not love God more than I loved my husband or my daughter.

As I sought God and prayed for healing, though, I learned what it meant to love Him like that. Despite my suffering, I stood in awe of His goodness. I claimed my identity as His adored daughter. My pain and weakness were temporary and somehow insignificant. It was no longer my first thought when I woke up. Instead, I eagerly anticipated spending time with my Father.

During that time, I heard a Christian speaker talking about this idea. He said, "We get so caught up in asking God for things. 'God, if you'll just give me this, if you'll just heal this, if you'll just get me this job, if you'll just save my marriage...' Why do we do that? We just need to ask for more of Jesus. When Jesus walks in the room, you get everything." That was a fundamental shift for me.

Over the months, I probably had people pray for me fifty times. I prayed for my own healing daily, usually many times a day. After all of that praying for healing and seeing none, I finally realized I already had the greatest blessing. My prayer changed. Instead of only praying for healing, I also prayed, "Father, if you never heal me, if I can just know you this way for the rest of my life, I'm satisfied. Having a relationship with you overshadows even the most difficult circumstances in my life."

Shortly afterward, I went to a prayer and deliverance ministry where a woman prayed and talked with me for hours. Driving home, I felt different. However, it had been such a long process that I did not want to falsely believe I had been healed. Nevertheless, I noticed in the coming days a renewed strength as I was going about my daily tasks. I could walk up and down the stairs without losing my breath. I could do the laundry with ease. I felt normal.

I went back to the prayer and deliverance ministry one more time to confirm my suspicions. I was lying on the floor, praying, weeping with the gravity of it all. I asked God, "Did you heal me? Are we finished with this chapter?" I felt Him respond, *Yes, it is finished.*

As I left, I called my husband and my family to tell them the news. They reacted with tentative excitement. "That's great," they said. "You should get tested!"

I went back to the doctor, the same one who had diagnosed me and prescribed the treatment regimen to address my multitude of problems. He tested me and found, to his surprise, the Lyme disease was gone. Not only that, but so were the co-infections for which I had barely started medications. Those treatments, he said, were not taken long enough to have been effective at eradicating the infections. Most amazingly, the intestinal parasites, for which I never took a single pill, were gone as well.

Through my trial, I earnestly prayed for healing, but God first wanted to give me something better: the greater blessing of understanding my relationship with Him as His adored daughter. The reality of my communion with God superseded the reality of my physical pain. Just as a girl values a present less than the father who gives it, I treasure the gift of miraculous healing less than the intimacy I gained with my Father.

CHAPTER SEVENTEEN

Convicted

I'm Nick, and this is my true story.

Nick

In high school, my identity was based on all the wrong things: sports, girls, drugs. I found myself in an unhealthy relationship filled with selfishness and sexual immorality. On top of that, I started cheating on my girlfriend. I lived recklessly and thoughtlessly. Even though I had grown up around church, I was about as far from being a believer as possible.

The transformation began one night when my friends and I were hanging out and smoking marijuana. After getting high, I offered to drive some of them home. They agreed and we made our way across town, but then I got pulled over. I was arrested and charged with driving under the influence of drugs and numerous counts of minor in possession.

I had to go to court multiple times. The first time, I learned about the possible consequences: approximately

$15,000 in fines, six months in a juvenile detention center, or about 800 hours of community service. The magnitude of the consequences overwhelmed me. It seemed like it would take an eternity to atone for what I had done. I dreaded my next visit to court, when everything would be final.

At my sentencing, the judge read my charges, each one out loud. He reminded me of the consequences I faced. He looked at me intently and asked, "How do you plead to these charges?"

"Guilty," I said.

The judge kept his gaze. He was silent. After a moment, he looked down at his papers. "You know what," he said, "I'm going to drop your charges and let you go free like it never happened."

I was stunned. I had never experienced such grace from a stranger. I could not believe the judge had offered this mercy. I deserved that penalty. I was living a life destined for punishment, but the judge spared me. Now that the judge had shown me such grace, I could not imagine returning to my selfish, empty life. How could I spit in the face of a man who gave me this second chance?

Elated, I shared this story with many people. One of them was my Young Life leader, a man whom I did not know well at the time. As I finished the story, he was beaming. "Dude," he said, "that's the gospel!"

That was the moment I understood what Jesus did for me. However, I noticed some astonishing differences between the judge and Jesus. Firstly, God knows about much more than a DUID and some MIPs; He knows about every single sin I have ever committed. Secondly, He did not drop my charges – He paid them. Because He is perfectly just, my sins required payment. But because He is perfectly loving and gracious, He paid my penalty with His own death.

That realization is what brought me to Christ and predicated the rest of these stories.

As I have journeyed through my faith, I have always wanted to see God do amazing things in people's lives. I believe in the power of prayer. I believe in miracles. I prayed for over three years for these things to happen in my life; I wanted God to use me to bring miracles to others. For years, though, nothing. I had many seasons of doubting, but eventually I came to an undeniable solution to my doubts: I could not ignore what the Bible said about God's nature and what we can do with the Holy Spirit. I realized my wrestling with God was not a bad thing. In that struggle, I was building intimacy with Him, learning more about Him, and strengthening my resilience.

The following year was a season of harvest. Though I had been praying for people's healing for over three years, this past year is the first time I have seen miraculous results from my prayers. But sometimes in God's Kingdom, when it rains, it pours. Before the harvest, though, I had one more lesson to learn.

***

In March of 2018, I went on a mission trip to Brazil. I was a part of a ministry team there that planned to visit several different churches. The main speaker would give a message and ask if anyone had pain or needed prayer for anything. Then the prayer team, including me, would pray for anyone who volunteered. I was excited to be a part of the team, and I believed that God was going to bring amazing healing.

When we arrived, we could not contain our excitement. Even though we planned to attend a church soon, we had some extra time, so we decided to pray for people on the street. My translator and I found a woman sitting alone. As we talked with her, we learned she was blind. My adrenaline surged – would God heal the blindness of the first person I prayed for? I prayed fervently, believing that God could heal her. However, her blindness did not go away. I kept praying, stopping, and then asking her if she could see, but she kept telling me she could not. The last time I asked her, tears were streaming down her face as she shook her head softly. "Why do you care so much?" she asked me.

"Because God loves you so much. He died for me when I didn't deserve it. He died for you, too. Now that I know Him, I know He wants me to share His love with others. I care about you because He told me to."

"Tell me more," she said. I proceeded to share the gospel with her. After a few moments, convicted by God's love for her and her need of Him, she accepted Jesus! I had gone into that interaction praying for a healing, but my concept of healing was too small, too temporal. God answered, over-delivering an eternal redemption rather than a physical healing! In retrospect, though, God did use that interaction to heal blindness: mine. It opened my eyes to the fact that my first priority should be the soul, not the body. It should be Him, not healing.

With a newfound focus and depth of purpose, I was excited when we arrived at our first Brazilian church, a small building packed with people. It was hot and smelled like sweat, but there was a tangible excitement in the air. The presence of God was thick. We expected the miraculous. The time for harvest had come.

The moment came. The speaker asked if anyone needed prayer. Several hands went up. My heart beat faster as I made my way toward a small woman between twenty and thirty years old. She explained, through my translator, that her stomach was in deep pain. She showed me bruises, but she did not explain how she got them.

After asking permission, I put my hand on her stomach and prayed for healing. The bruises disappeared instantly before our eyes. As she sobbed, I realized this was one of the most beautiful moments of my life. She embraced me, still sobbing and rambling excitedly in Portuguese. I laughed, unable to understand, and simply said, "Praise the Lord!"

Later in the service, the same woman came back to me with a translator. She fell on her knees, sobbing again. She explained the bruises on her stomach had been from her abusive husband. That is why her reaction was so strong when God healed her. She felt much more than a physical healing. She experienced an emotional and spiritual healing. God had used her physical miracle to set her free from that relationship. God had shown her He sees her pain and He cares for her. He had proven to her that He was not only the God of the universe – He was also the God of her heart.

She excitedly told me she wanted to do this for other people and asked me to impart the gift of healing to her. Of course, the gift of healing comes from the Holy

Spirit, but I prayed with her anyway, and she left with a new sense of freedom, purpose, and power.

In another church on the same mission trip, we were in a similar service when a middle-aged man in glasses approached me to ask for prayer. Through my translator, I learned he was blind in his right eye. The vision in his left eye was not much better.

As I learned through his translator about his condition, it was unclear how much, if any, vision he had in his right eye, so I asked him to cover his left eye with his hand. He did, and I held up three fingers about six inches from his face. "Can you see my hand?"

"No," he responded, "I can see a little white dot in the middle, but everything else is black."

We prayed and asked for healing. Every few minutes, I tested him again. For the first five or ten minutes, nothing seemed to be happening. I was getting discouraged, but we persevered. Eventually, he could correctly identify how many fingers I was holding six inches from his face.

We continued praying. I tested him again, this time a foot from his face. He could answer correctly, but as I moved my hand further away, he could not tell how many fingers I held up. We prayed again. I moved two feet away. He could now answer correctly. More prayer.

Now five feet. More prayer. Eventually, he was twenty feet away or more and was able to answer correctly!

As I reflected on the incident afterwards, I remembered something I had not realized in the intensity of the moment. Before that church service, I had been talking with one of my friends and told her, "I just want to see God do something amazing tonight, a big miracle!" We had prayed, and she had specifically asked that I would witness someone who was blind be able to see.

Talking with some other members of my group after the service, I learned the blind man seeing was not the only amazing healing to take place during that time. Across the room, at the same time I was praying for the blind man, my friend Mike was praying for a man named Marcos.

Marcos approached Mike with the help of his walker; he was immobile without it. They sat together, and Marcos explained to Mike that he used to be a professional snowboarder and breakdancer, but he had been in a devastating car accident which had left him paralyzed from the neck down.

During his first surgery, Marcos explained, he had been visited by Jesus. Marcos was not a Christian beforehand, but Jesus had appeared to him and explained His own gospel. Immediately when he woke up from his surgery, Marcos had dedicated his life to Jesus.

After his second surgery to address his mobility, during which Jesus visited Marcos again, he had some movement in his legs. Unfortunately, he was not able to support his body weight. For the first three to four months after the surgery, physical therapy seemed to be helping. Then his progress stalled. Five months of physical therapy with no real improvement. Marcos tried to understand. He began to believe that perhaps this was his 'cross to bear,' punishment for some sin in his past. He had to atone for this sin, and his handicap was how he would atone.

After hearing this, Mike began to encourage Marcos and explain God's nature to him. Mike told him, "That is a lie. You do not need to bear this 'cross.'" As they talked, Marcos changed his perspective and relinquished his former belief he would forever be a paralytic.

Then they started praying. Periodically, Marcos tested his legs by moving them as he sat. Little by little, Marcos felt his mobility returning.

Suddenly, he announced he wanted to try walking. He was wobbly as he rose to his feet. People helped him to walk up and down the aisle, but he soon wanted to do it by himself. Then for the first time in nine months, he walked unassisted up and down the aisle, then around the entire church sanctuary.

A blind man seeing and a lame man walking – all in a day's work for God!

As we continued on our mission trip, I noticed our local translators seemed to think we Americans had some sort of advantage in making miracles happen. The Brazilians I met did not feel equipped to pray for miracles; they did not know how.

I looked for an opportunity to empower my translator and found it when a woman approached us during a church service. She told us she had cancer, pointing to a lump on her back. "Why don't you pray for her?" I asked my translator.

She was hesitant at first, but I encouraged her and told her to put her hand on the lump. I put my hand on hers and helped her with the prayer. "In Jesus' name, we command this lump and this disease to be gone." Immediately, we felt it vanish.

It changed the way my translator thought about herself. It helped her to understand that, like any Christian, she has full-time access to the Holy Spirit. She does not need earthly permission or training – she needs faith and willingness to pray for miracles.

As I thought about the event later, I realized this is what Jesus did with the disciples. While He could have performed all of the miracles Himself, He left plenty of that work to them. I wonder if the church would have multiplied so quickly if Jesus had not empowered the disciples to carry the mantle He left them...

Despite the incredible experience I had in Brazil witnessing God's miracles, I came under attack when I returned to the United States. In retrospect, it sounds ridiculous, but I began to believe the lie that God does not perform miracles like that here in the U.S. I had been praying for healing and breakthrough for various people in my life, but it did not seem to be working. I wrestled with God. "Do you do big miracles here?" His answer came one day at the rock climbing gym where I work.

I have a coworker named Rachel who used to play competitive softball. As a result of her playing, she had a chronic problem with her right shoulder. Any time she climbed for more than about fifteen minutes, her shoulder would flare up and start to hurt.

When she mentioned it to me one day as it began to bother her, I looked at her back and could see her right shoulder was noticeably lower than her left. "Let's pray," I suggested.

We prayed once, and immediately she exclaimed, "The pain is gone!" She mentioned her shoulder felt hot where the pain had been. I saw her shoulders were still not lined up, so I decided to pray again. Nothing seemed to change, but she remarked again that her shoulder was very hot and the pain was completely gone.

A few weeks later, she approached me with a huge smile. "Nick, my shoulder hasn't hurt at all since you prayed for me!"

It strikes me that this is the story of my life, too. Externally, I still look like the broken vessel I was before my salvation, askew and imperfect, but God has changed me inside. While I maintain some of my earthly flaws, I am free to climb, and I do so in pursuit of the ultimate prize: eternity in Heaven with Jesus and lots of friends up there with me!

CHAPTER EIGHTEEN

City of Jerusalem

We're Oscar, Annie, Jonathan, and Alejandro, and this is our true story.

Oscar

Jonathan

Oscar

About two years ago, in the week leading up to Easter Sunday, our church produced an immersive, walk-through experience sharing the life and death of Jesus. We had a field next to the church where we built tall walls and corridors that would take groups of twenty to thirty people through ten scenes. The entire production was offered in Spanish and English. Due to the massive scale of the project, it took over a year to plan, coordinate, and execute.

We had endless paperwork and permits, but it was worth all the time and money we put into it. The first year was a smashing success, seeing over eight hundred people journey through our miniature Jerusalem. We received overwhelmingly positive feedback as well, so we planned to make it a regular event occurring every two years.

This year, we decided to scale it up even further. We increased our budget and expanded our marketing. We built a bigger, better city. Our efforts paid off: pre-registrations projected up to fifteen hundred attendees.

Actors and directors planned and rehearsed their scenes months in advance. One of the scenes focused on the suicide of Judas, the disciple who betrayed Jesus for money and then hung himself. Among our team, it was a controversial scene; some believed it was too graphic. When we interviewed attendees from the first year's production, though, they said it was one of the most memorable and impactful scenes, so we eventually decided to keep it in the program.

This year, the English-speaking Judas would be played by David, who had performed both languages in the first year's production. There was a new Spanish-speaking Judas this year though: Javier, a lanky, shy young man who had recently moved to the United States from Cuba and dreamed of becoming a doctor. He came to the United States alone, so the church became his second family. Most of us viewed him as a kind but mischievous little brother.

Javier started attending almost every church event and volunteering whenever he could. He helped with the youth group and joined the worship team. Everyone in the church knew him and loved him, a genuine, playful young man who loved to joke around.

Javier was excited to participate, and he fully committed to his performance. Javier even grew out his beard and hair for the part; he wanted to look a little crazed and desperate. Javier was so dedicated to his role that when he and David practiced, David and his brother Jonathan sometimes had to tell Javier to make his performance less intense. The hanging could easily be too graphic, especially with Javier's enthusiasm. Nevertheless, Javier and David were ready for their performances, committed to their roles. We were all ready. Our plan was grand, and we had done everything we could to prepare. However, God had planned something else entirely.

Opening night. It was Friday, a week before Good Friday. As the sun set, my wife Annie and I took our places – she was a group guide, and I was putting participants in groups. The first Spanish group arrived and awaited entry. Things got started a little later than expected though, so we ended up combining the first two Spanish-speaking groups together.

Annie

I was an English group guide, assigned the task of leading a group through all ten scenes. The guides who were not actively leading groups were pre-assigned to be extras in certain scenes. When I arrived on the day of the first performance and they told me where I had been assigned, I was disappointed because my kids were actors in a different scene. If I had asked to be reassigned, they probably would have moved me to the scene with my kids, but for some reason I did not say anything.

People began arriving to watch the performances. The first group was Spanish-speaking. When we heard the second group was English-speaking, another guide and I discussed who would lead them. It was her first time, and she had told me before that she was nervous to lead her first group, so I volunteered. "I'll do it," I told her.

"No, that's okay," she said. "I just want to do it instead of waiting and getting more nervous."

"Are you sure?" I asked.

"Definitely."

If I had been assigned to the scene with my children or if I had led the first English-speaking group, I would have been in a completely different part of the city of Jerusalem. God planned it so I would be available when and where He wanted to use me.

Jonathan

I was jittery as the night began. Normally, I was a worship leader. Tonight, though, I was part of the marketing team – this debut was the culmination of my hard work and the work of countless others. Plus, my brother David was the English-speaking actor for the Judas scene. He performed wonderfully two years ago, and I was excited to see him again. I had been praying and preparing for this event for months, and it was finally here.

The first group that entered was a Spanish-speaking group. I waited to go through with the English-speaking group for whom my brother would perform. As we went through the journey, the first three scenes went well, but then something strange happened: we stalled. We stood idle, waiting for about ten minutes. It was awkward, and I was frustrated because I felt this would detract from people's experience. My frustration turned to anger when I heard the sirens of passing ambulances and police cars. We were meant to seamlessly move through from scene to scene, immersed in the story. Stopping interrupted the effect, but the sirens ruined it entirely. "God, first we stall and then we have sirens interrupting the performances? Why would this happen?" But then I noticed that the sirens were not passing. They had gotten louder, then steady. Then the sirens silenced.

Things worsened when a pastor approached our group. "I'm sorry, but we need everyone to exit the city. We had an incident – police are here."

Alejandro

I was excited about helping with this year's City of Jerusalem production. I had experience helping with sound and lights during our regular church services, which was fun, but helping with a scene in our pre-Easter production was different and felt more intense than a normal weekend service. During a weekend service, I would show up to practice, log into the computer (the password was the church's address), and sit there, adjusting sound dials or pressing buttons to activate lighting cues. In the City of Jerusalem, though, I had to crouch down in a dark corner behind a set piece, barely obscured from the audience. It was gripping and theatrical, and the effect would be lost if I missed my cues or if I were seen.

We had different sound people scheduled for each scene. On the day of the first performance, one of the coordinators called me and told me there was a last-minute change. I had originally been scheduled to run sound for the crucifixion scene, but the middle-schooler who had been scheduled for the Judas scene was not feeling well. The coordinator needed me to take his place. I was excited to be stationed there; I had heard it was a powerful scene, and my friend Javier was the lead actor for the Spanish-speaking groups.

Talking with him beforehand, I knew Javier was nervous to perform his first scene. I encouraged him right before the first group arrived and then hurried to my spot. I could hear people walking in, shuffling to the viewing area in front of where Javier would perform. The scene began, and Javier was doing wonderfully. His lines were convincing, his delivery confident.

My heart beat faster as we approached the end of the scene: the climax when Judas would hang himself. Earlier, Javier had shown me how the illusion worked. He would place the noose around his neck, but it would not tighten. He would then step off of a platform onto a lower platform which was obscured from the audience's view. Despite its simplicity, it looked incredibly convincing from the audience's perspective, especially when Javier leaned forward and swung slightly from side to side.

The moment arrived. Javier delivered his final line, placing the noose around his neck. He stepped from the platform and hung. It was extremely convincing. Lowering the music, I could hear the guttural noises he made and the thumping of his body against the wall next to him as he twitched. I had an uneasy feeling that something was wrong, but for some reason, I was frozen. As Javier's theatrics slowly decrescendoed, I could hear the gory silence of the audience. They stood there watching for what felt like a long time, waiting for a signal to move on. None came, so they eventually shuffled out, much more slowly now than when they entered.

Once the last of them left and everything was quiet, I emerged from my hiding spot and ran to him, calling out, "Javier, are you okay?" No response. In the darkness, his body swayed slightly, silently. I prodded him and asked again, "Are you okay?" Nothing. Frantically, I tried to lift his body and remove the noose, but I struggled to do both at the same time. After a couple of attempts, I was finally able to release Javier's body from the noose. Just then, David was coming around the corner to see how Javier's first performance had gone. He raced toward me and helped me to lower Javier's body. We pulled him out to the viewing area where the audience had been and laid his body down.

As we tried to bring him to consciousness, I could see Javier's eyes were rolled back in his head and his tongue was sticking out slightly. From a lifeguarding course I had taken recently, I knew how to check for a pulse. What they did not explain is what it feels like when someone does not have one. I was not prepared for that feeling. When I checked Javier, I felt nothing but a sickening stillness in his veins.

Annie

Since I did not have a group and would not get one for a while, I headed to my scene to be an extra. On my way there, I met one of the other guides. Since I was momentarily unoccupied, she asked me, "Annie, will you tell Javier not to perform his scene so realistically? Some of the guests found it too disturbing."

"Sure," I said, heading toward Javier's station. As I approached, I saw Jonathan and David pulling Javier out into the audience viewing area. He was completely limp. My body pulsed with adrenaline. I am a nurse, so I am trained to handle emergency situations. However, it is much different when the victim is someone you know and the context is somewhere other than work.

What happened next was a whirlwind. In my memory, it feels like a dream where I watch everything take place. I was not in control; the Holy Spirit took over. I ran to Javier and told the people around him, "Let me take a look at him." One of them produced a phone and shined light onto Javier. I will never forget his face, completely lifeless and gray. In my medical training, I had learned when a person lacked oxygen, they would turn cyanotic, meaning bluish. Javier was far past that point.

I checked to see if he was breathing. He was not. I felt for a pulse – none. I smelled feces, a sign his body had released his bowels, which happens when people die. Stunned, I looked at his lifeless face and limp body. Dead.

Alejandro

By now, Annie had arrived on scene as well. As I took a moment to stand back and register what was happening, I remembered something else I learned in my lifeguarding course. They said that often in an emergency situation, people are so panicked they do not call 911. I immediately reached for my phone and dialed as I moved toward the exit of the city. I described to the operator what had happened and she asked me for the address, which I supplied.

It was not until much later that I realized how God had prepared me for that night and orchestrated my presence there. The middle-schooler who was originally scheduled to run sound for that scene was much younger and smaller than me. He would have been far more traumatized by the event, but he also was not large enough to get Javier down from the noose. He also was not part of our lighting team at church, so he would not have known the church's address. In fact, very few people knew the church's address offhand. Finally, that middle-schooler did not have my training and likely would not have called 911.

Annie

Despite the fact I knew Javier was dead, I felt obligated to begin chest compressions – I could not just stand there and do nothing. However, compressions are incredibly tiring to perform, especially the longer they are required. I needed help. There was one other member of our volunteer team who I knew had CPR training because he was a firefighter.

I called his name in the desperate hope he would be within earshot. It was unlikely – the city corridors were designed to transmit as little sound as possible between scenes, and the city was huge, half the size of a football field. A hundred volunteers were spread throughout it; unless he were nearby, there was no way the firefighter would hear me. Miraculously, right as I called, he was walking up behind me. We alternated performing compressions until some police officers arrived and took over.

It was not until I stepped back from Javier's body that I fully realized what had happened. I began weeping. I could not believe this night that had been planned to bring people to Jesus had been corrupted by the accidental death of one of our church members. My head began swirling and the walls began tightening, squeezing the breath from my lungs. Fragmented thoughts assaulted me. His family. Our church. The community. What if? Why? How? Anger. Fear. Most of all, sorrow for my friend who had left us.

Jonathan

As we exited the city, a woman from my church approached me. She was weeping as she buried her face in my chest. "I don't know what happened," she said, "but Javier hung himself while he was doing his scene."

I was in disbelief. I had seen Javier and David practice the scene before; I knew exactly how the effect worked. The rope would be taut after the actor stepped down, but the noose would not tighten. It would not affect the actor's ability to breathe. Nevertheless, I watched the ambulance arrive and saw the EMTs take Javier's lifeless body from the scene.

My brother David ran out from the city and fell to his knees in the parking lot. He told me later that he was praying for resurrection. He knew Javier was dead; David had no illusions about his condition. He had helped move Javier's limp body from the platform. David had watched as Alejandro and Annie discovered he was not breathing and had no pulse. He had looked on as they performed CPR on Javier's unresponsive body for several minutes.

Annie

The police closed the entire area off; they believed this may be a crime scene. Police cars blocked the exit of the parking lot and officers watched to ensure no one left. They began to interview everyone who had been closely involved with Javier or the scene. As the rest of us waited, people began to gather in the parking lot and pray.

I had never seen my church pray that way, with such earnest abandon. In the darkness, I could see over a hundred dwarfed bodies on their knees, on their faces. Many were members of our church, but many were from the community. Even unbelievers were audibly crying out to God for Javier's life. The night air was filled with beautifully tragic wails and whispers, sobs and shouts. The sound was sobering. All of the chaos that had been swirling in my mind came into focus. This was what mattered: our brother died, but we had a loving Father. We needed to cry out to Him. In doing that, we came together as one organism, one family. How could our loving Father not be moved as so many of His children pleaded with Him?

Most people had only heard pieces of the story – they knew Javier had accidentally hanged himself, that he was taken away in an ambulance – but they did not know the extent of his condition. They had hope that God could keep him from dying. I did not have the heart to tell them Javier was already dead.

Javier's lifeless face flashed in my mind as I prayed. My prayers were different from most of the people in the parking lot. I prayed that God would help us in the aftermath. "Help us with the grieving process, comfort those who mourn. Help us with the funeral arrangements."

Jonathan

I saw people gathering in the parking lot to pray and joined in the assembly of the desperate. After a while, a pastor suggested we go into the church sanctuary. Another pastor led us in prayer. I have never prayed so intently in my life, nor have I ever been surrounded by others who so fervently requested the same hopeless outcome.

A pastor pulled me aside. He asked me to go up to the sound booth and choose a worship song. I reluctantly agreed and begrudgingly ascended the steps. That was the last thing I wanted to do in that moment. How could I worship a God who just allowed my friend to die? A God who had allowed it to occur in front of an audience, during the debut performance for a massive ministry we have slaved months to produce? I continued out of blind obedience. I did not know what else to do.

As we sang, I saw people come together and lay their confusion, anger, hopelessness, and pain before the Lord. It was awe-inspiring. Some sang loudly, forcing themselves to praise through their sobs. Some sang quietly between sniffles, in reverent submission. Some simply stood with eyes closed and faces turned upwards, tears streaming down. Some knelt in silence. The consensus was praise despite the affliction. If these people could open their wounded hearts to the God who had seemingly turned His back, so could I.

In the following moments as I sang to Him, I felt the undeniable presence of my Father as He embraced me. It was like the embraces loved ones share at a memorial service, those long embraces where you hold one another and weep. The embrace does not change what happened or take the pain away, but it says, *I am so sorry we are going through this. I love you, and we are in this together. I am here for you no matter what.*

Annie

Later that night, we received news they had found a pulse. My heart sank. We had calculated that Javier went at least eight to ten minutes without oxygen. Clinically, the body can only last four to five minutes without permanent brain damage. Javier would certainly be in a vegetative state; the damage to his brain would be extensive and irreparable. After I learned they had found a pulse, my prayers changed. "God, if Javier is going to be brain-dead, please just take him home to be with you."

I continued to wrestle with God, struggling with the fact He allowed this to happen. Eventually, I was able to pray, "God, you are sovereign. You allowed this to happen, but I know you have a plan. I know you love us. Please be with us and show us your love and goodness." I thought about when Jesus died on the cross and the hopelessness His family and friends felt as a result. But the darkest moment in human history preceded its total redemption and brought us our greatest blessing.

Jonathan

In the days following, I had the opportunity to talk with some of the people who were in the audience for Javier's performance. Some of them were doctors and nurses, people who could have saved Javier's life. However, they described an unexplainable feeling of paralysis as they watched him hang. They had a sinking feeling something was wrong, but they were frozen in place, unable to rush to his aid. When the group had finally moved onward, something had kept them from intervening, although one of them did tell a guide it seemed disturbingly realistic. As they were talking with me later, each of those people described a deep shame and regret for not having done something to help.

Annie

The next day, on Saturday, we continued to pray throughout the day. We heard Javier had been moving slightly, but we knew those could simply be muscle spasms. The church gathered for a special prayer service for Javier. Later that day, we received news Javier was reacting to people in his hospital room. People would say, "If you can hear me, squeeze my hand," and he would! It was impossible, but it was evidence he had at least some brain function.

Jonathan

I had to lead worship for the Sunday service, just two days after Javier's accident. As I planned the songs, I held onto our scrap of hope: Javier had squeezed someone's hand. I found songs about God's promises, His faithfulness, His help in times of trouble.

During the second service on Sunday, we received news Javier had woken up from his coma! When we announced the news to the church, their response was pure joy – ear-splitting, floor-shaking, undignified praise. The worship that weekend, especially after Javier woke up, was unforgettable. The congregation sang those songs as a genuine response, a reflection of what their hearts were experiencing. God keeps his promises. He is faithful. He is good and loving. It reminded me of the Israelites' response after they witnessed the parting of the Red Sea.

Annie

On Sunday afternoon, they extubated Javier and he was eating! Over the next few hours, we received more updates: he was talking and laughing. On Monday, we went to visit him in the hospital. When I walked into the room, his eyes met mine and he smiled. He glanced down for a second to think, as though he were searching for my name in his bedsheets. I noticed the purple markings around the front of his neck where the rope had been. Javier looked at me again. "Annie!" he said.

Jonathan

When I visited Javier in the hospital soon after the accident, I asked him what he remembered. He could recall very little, so he said with a grin, "I just remember eating some bad soup that made my stomach ache and that's why I'm here!" When I heard that, I knew my friend was back from the dead. I had worried he would not be the same, that my friend was gone, but this was the Javier I knew, the lovable jokester.

Alejandro

I went to visit Javier in the hospital on Monday. When I arrived, I learned to my astonishment he was going to be released from the ICU later that day. A doctor even commented to me, "Nobody gets out of the ICU in three days, especially after something like this!"

Jonathan

Through the trauma of Javier's death and the miracle afterward, we realized many things. We realized how little faith we had. We realized God's power to answer even those prayers we believed were impossible.

We saw God's care and comfort for us even as we were grieving. Most of all, we gained an experiential, unshakeable knowledge that God is real, alive, present, and loving.

Reflecting, I think about those people in the audience who watched Javier be hanged but felt paralyzed. I believe God prevented them from intervening. God did not want them to save Javier because God wanted to resurrect him. God did not want this to be a story about a heroic doctor or nurse – He wanted this to be a story about a heroic God.

When the accident happened, we shut down the City of Jerusalem experience. After the miracle, though, the pastors discussed the possibility of opening it again and finishing the last few nights of planned performances before Easter Sunday. City officials would not allow it. They had revoked our permits, increasing the previous requirements. Instead of meeting the requirements for a temporary structure, we would now have to meet building and electrical codes for a permanent structure. Even if we had had the manpower and knowhow to do the work required, it was cost-prohibitive.

We had to contact those who had registered and tell them what had happened, but it gave us an opportunity to share the miracle as well. News spread. Our church and the community members who were there could not stop talking about it. Even a food truck vendor who was there told his family in Greece! It was as though God did not want us to continue the performances because He did not want anything distracting from the miracle He had just performed. God had already achieved more using our Jerusalem city than our performances would accomplish. It was enough. It was finished.

Easter Sunday, 10 days after Javier's death. On the day celebrating the greatest miracle ever performed, we had another reason to celebrate. As a familiar song played through the speakers, I could not help but think how God had played a familiar song through Javier's miracle. God had composed miracles of resurrection in Biblical times, and now he had reprised resurrection for us. My heart swelled. I could feel myself on the verge of tears, tears of gratitude and wonder. Then the doors in the back opened. The congregation cheered as I began to laugh and cry at the same time. Javier was walking down the aisle to join our church family in the service celebrating our resurrected Lord.

To hear more from Annie, check out *Simple Faith by Annie* on YouTube and Instagram!

Javier today

CHAPTER NINETEEN

Papa

I'm Lee, and this is the latest part of my true story.

Over eight years ago, my wife and I got married. Although it was an amazing time of celebration, it was also tinged with dread. Shortly before our wedding, Amy's grandpa, "Papa," had a scare with prostate cancer.

Little did we know God would use that experience with prostate cancer to reveal to Papa that he was in the advanced stages of heart failure. Although his heart showed evidence of multiple heart attacks, he had not felt them; it took the prostate cancer episode for doctors to learn Papa needed surgery for his heart to keep beating. Only a few days before our wedding, Papa was scheduled for triple bypass open heart surgery. He had a fifty percent chance of survival.

Amy and her Papa had always shared a special bond. As the family tells it, God used Amy, Papa's first granddaughter, to touch Papa's heart in a new way. When he met Amy at the hospital where she was born, something in him softened. He suddenly became tenderer, more sentimental. He cried more, he smiled more.

He never lost his edge, though. Papa was brilliant, always up on the latest technology and able to talk business or sports with anyone. He had a quick wit, too. He laughed easily and loved to make others smile. A master of comedic timing and a novice at political correctness, Papa loved to ride the line between inappropriate and hilarious.

I did not know Papa very well before I married Amy, but my heart broke for my bride. Surely God would not allow her adored Papa to leave us right before his first grandchild got married.

Much of Amy's family managed to visit Papa just a few days before our wedding. In that time, many of them said things to him they had never said before. However, they came back with heavy hearts. They were unsure if Papa knew Jesus.

All of us were praying.

The surgery went well, thank God. They also installed a pacemaker to mitigate future issues that may arise. Bedridden during recovery, Papa was unable to attend our wedding, but he would have more time with us.

The next seven years were some of the fullest years of Papa's life. A lover of baseball, Papa attended literally hundreds of baseball games played by his youngest grandson, Ryan. Through those seasons, Papa and Ryan communicated almost daily, encouraging and inspiring one another. Papa knew all of the players and coaches by name, as well as many of the players on the other teams. For countless people, Papa's positive paternal influence provided an example of what really matters on the baseball diamond.

The most important event during those seven years happened at a church service about a year and a half ago. Papa and Grandma (we are now close enough that I call them both by these names) were in town visiting. Whenever they could, Papa and Grandma attended our church if Amy and I were singing. Papa sometimes even cheered just like at Ryan's baseball games.

After a rousing sermon, the pastor ended his message with an altar call. Even though he had told everyone to close their eyes, Amy and her sister Erin peeked and saw Papa raise his hand. Finally, we had the assurance we had all prayed for: Papa would be with us in Heaven.

A few months later, Papa and Grandma moved just twenty minutes from where Amy and I live, and they were excited to attend church with us each weekend. They quickly settled in. Papa and Grandma even had a usual spot, seven rows back on the right side. If they could not attend for any reason, they would stream the service online or watch the recording later.

Soon after they moved here, Papa and Grandma were planning a vacation with Amy's parents. They were all eagerly anticipating the trip. They had been talking about it nonstop for weeks.

The morning of the trip, Papa was ready early, as usual. A few minutes before it was time to leave, he was bending down to tie his shoes when his heart went into fibrillation, causing his defibrillator to deliver a massive shock. He likely would have died if he had not had an internal defibrillator device. That set into motion several months of emergencies, hospital stays, and surgeries as the doctors attempted to delay his inevitable decline. "Hearts don't get better," the doctors kept telling us.

Papa increasingly suffered from ventricular tachycardia (VT), a problem that prevented enough blood from reaching his brain, causing him to pass out almost without warning. After falling and breaking his ankle during one of those episodes, Papa grew much more cautious.

The only viable solution to the VT was an ablation procedure. It was risky, but Papa was living in constant fear of falling. He was mostly confined to his chair. An ablation seemed like the only option, so he decided to take the risk. When the doctors performed the procedure, they ablated well over 150 sites in his heart, an unusually high number over three times the average.

He survived the procedure, but it was unsuccessful. Papa continued to be plagued with VT. To make matters worse, given his advancing congestive heart failure, surgically installing an LVAD device seemed to be his best chance for long-term survival. Unless he received this device, the doctors predicted he would live less than a year, and his quality of life would continue worsening. Unfortunately, he was not eligible for the LVAD device unless the VT was under control, meaning he would have to undergo another risky ablation procedure.

The first time he received an ablation, Papa was in pretty good health overall. In fact, almost all of the doctors and nurses commented on how good he looked for an advanced congestive heart failure patient. Perhaps because he still looked so strong, perhaps because we were naive, we had hardly grasped the severity of Papa's first ablation procedure. Plus, as he frequently reminded us, Papa was a "tough old hide," seemingly immune to the dangers around him. As his second ablation approached, though, the tone was grave. We now realized it could fail, and months more of VT and a sedentary lifestyle had taken their toll on Papa. Fewer doctors and nurses commented on how good Papa looked.

The ablation was to take place in Denver, where the foremost doctors in the field would supervise and conduct the procedure. We planned to make a family weekend of it. We wanted to support Grandma, and for the first time in about 8 years, it felt like a real possibility Papa might leave us.

The night before the procedure, the family gathered in the hotel lobby, and we said a prayer together. We rose early the next morning after a restless night and convened in the hospital waiting room. Then we waited. The doctors called Grandma with an update every two hours. "He's doing well," they would tell us. "Everything is going smoothly!"

They finished later than expected. The doctor, tired from the work but optimistic, greeted us in the waiting room. "The procedure went well. There was one minor complication: something similar to a bruise appeared on the heart's wall during the ablation. We'll be keeping a close eye on it. It could be a serious problem if it grows, but right now there is no cause for concern."

We celebrated and went out for dinner that night. The next morning, we went to the hospital together. We awaited an update from the doctors. They seemed to take hours to get to us, perhaps because of their other cases, perhaps because they were trying to find a way to deliver what they had to say next.

Six or seven doctors with inscrutable faces filed into Papa's room. As they entered, most of them kept their eyes fixed on the floor, even once the lead doctor finally spoke. She explained the "bruise" was actually called a pseudoaneurysm. It meant there was a hole through at least one layer of his heart's wall. If it grew, it would likely mean Papa's death.

Unfortunately, initial readings seemed to indicate the pseudoaneurysm was slowly growing and bleeding. The only way for Papa to survive was to maintain a tenuous balance between keeping his blood thick enough to hopefully clot over the pseudoaneurysm but not so thick that unwanted clots formed and caused strokes.

To make matters worse, they explained, Papa's heart was so enlarged, stressed, and stretched that it could rupture at any moment. If it did, he would die instantly. Miraculously though, past scarring on his heart had reinforced the area where the pseudoaneurysm had formed, preventing it from instantly causing a lethal rupture when it first appeared. Only one of the heart specialists in the hospital had ever seen someone survive

193

such an event, and that doctor had only seen one other in his entire career.

Nevertheless, they told us, we should not leave anything unsaid. We should notify family this might be the end. Death seemed a breath away. After we called the few family members who were not there already, we spent the next several hours praying, crying, and speaking the tenderest words I have ever heard my family utter. In that tragedy, our family built a bond closer than we had ever felt.

There were countless moments like this, but one such moment was when I stole some time to speak with Papa by his bedside. He looked into my eyes and said through choked-back tears, "You know I love you like my own flesh and blood, Lee."

"I know, Papa," I replied with my hand on his shoulder. "And you're my Papa, too. I love you, and I want you to know we're going to take care of Grandma when you're gone, whenever that is."

The hours ticked by as we awaited an alarm, a rush of nurses into the room. But Papa stayed. More family arrived. More indescribable moments, equal parts tragic and heavenly. In the days following that fateful news from the doctors, Papa was able to speak lucidly, intentionally, with all three of his daughters, all six of his grandchildren, and many other members of the family he built and blessed.

Between these conversations, we sought more prayer from our church family. We were surrounded by love and support from them in a way we had never experienced. In addition to the prayer, our church family called, texted, and offered to bring us things or take care of our pets at home. Two of our pastors even drove over an hour to visit us, encourage us, and pray with us during what we felt would be Papa's final hours.

Despite the fear, we all clung to hope that God would perform a miracle for Papa. Knowing I was writing this book, many people told Papa they were praying his story would make it into these pages. Papa was excited at the prospect. He made jokes about me having to interview him and trying to make him look good in his picture.

To be honest, though, I had reservations. Obviously, I fully believe in God's ability to perform miracles, but I also believe He does so according to His own will and timing. I feared if Papa were not miraculously saved, it may cause certain family members to doubt God's goodness, or perhaps His very existence.

The logical explanation of God's mysterious decisions about when to perform miracles is fairly simple (see the first chapter), but the heart speaks a different language. When a loving spouse of fifty-six years dies, no amount of head knowledge can fill the void. No answers can satisfy the questions.

This journey was terrifying for Grandma, filled with unknowns. Almost everything about her daily life would likely soon change. She would no longer come downstairs in the mornings to find Papa waiting for her in his favorite armchair. He would no longer look up at her, smile, and grumble, "Good morning" in his warm, gruff voice. They had made a great team, and Grandma could not help but realize she would have a lot to figure out on her own now that Papa would soon be gone.

Grandma tried to reconcile everything she was feeling. She sometimes seemed to be handling it shockingly well. Other times it would overwhelm her: sadness, anxiety, anger.

Hours turned to days. Still no alarms. Papa managed to continue hovering in the threadthin purgatory between bleeding out and having a stroke. We came to the end of our scheduled stay. After all, we had only expected to spend a couple of days there. We arranged to extend our visit. A day later, we had to reevaluate as we faced another extension. Our responsibilities beckoned.

Trying to make the right decision, I managed to intercept the lead doctor in the hallway. I probed for a recommendation. She was reluctant to offer any guidance because of all the unknowns. I explained my situation:

"We will do what we need to do, but we can't stay indefinitely. If we're looking at a couple of days, we will stay. If it will be a month, we'll go back and just visit as much as we can."

She hesitantly told me Papa could pass any time between now and a month from now. She would be very surprised if he lasted more than a month. I asked if there was any chance he could get better. She paused. She took a breath, looked into my eyes, and said in a low but confident voice, "There is a very, very small chance of anything good happening at this point." It was the most definite thing I had heard her say about Papa's prognosis. However, she ultimately recommended I go home.

Amy and much of her family stayed for another day or two. Still no alarms. The scans started showing the pseudoaneurysm was clotting. Soon, to everyone's surprise, Papa was released from the hospital. That in itself was a minor miracle. The doctors told him they would reevaluate him for an LVAD procedure after six to eight weeks of healing from the ablation.

Over the next few weeks, however, Papa had several medical emergencies and hospital visits. Even in that time, during his many hospital stays, he always made a point to learn everyone's names, thank them, and get to know them, from the doctors to the cleaning ladies. When he had time with them, he would ask them about their lives or brag to them about his family. He had even exchanged contact information with some of his favorite nurses, promising to take them out for coffee once this was all over.

Some nurses had mixed feelings about Papa, though. There were times when he was not supposed to use the bathroom by himself, but he once refused to go unless the nurse left the room. When she declined, he sweet-talked the doctor into making an exception, and the nurse just shook her head. Papa would tell that story with a chuckle, saying things like, "She didn't like me very much because I wouldn't let her watch me use the crapper." Another time, he pushed the same nurse even further when she had to draw blood or something. Just as the needle touched his skin, Papa feigned a loud yelp of pain. The nurse almost had a heart attack of her own – Papa laughed about that for days.

And then there are the things the nurses did not know about. My favorite was the day after Papa had been complaining about the "heart healthy" options on the hospital menu. One of his daughters smuggled in a donut for Papa, and he made an elaborate show of dramatically and conspicuously hiding it anytime someone walked by the open door. When a nurse actually did come in to check on him, he quickly tucked his half-eaten donut under his sheets, genuinely concerned he was going to get reprimanded. What he did not realize was that he had bits of glaze all around his mouth. Luckily, the nurse either decided not to say anything or did not notice. As soon as she left, he retrieved his treasured pastry and polished it off when the coast was clear.

That brings us to about two weeks ago.

Papa had been hospitalized again, and the doctors were trying to get his cocktail of medicines balanced. When we went to visit him, he looked different. He had lost so much weight over the past year; he looked like his own ghost. He was pale and clammy. No one commented on how good he looked. His outward appearance finally reflected the advanced stage of his heart failure. The worst part, though, was the look in his eyes. Up until now, he had maintained his sense of optimism. Now his eyes were filled with fatigue and despair. He felt out of options. From the information he had, his heart was not strong enough to handle an LVAD surgery. But continuing complications made it seem impossible he would ever become healthy enough for the surgery he needed. The change was palpable. Anyone looking at Papa could see his hopelessness was as lethal as anything he had yet faced.

Recognizing this, the doctors decided to move forward with the LVAD surgery despite the fact he was not an ideal candidate. It had been almost exactly six weeks, the minimum amount of time since his ablation for them to consider performing the procedure. As soon as he received the news, Papa's entire demeanor shifted. He had regained hope. There was one last chance.

The surgery was scheduled suddenly, and many of us were unable to be there. We talked with Papa on the phone the day before his surgery. He sounded like his old self. There was not much to say, though. We had already said everything that needed to be said. We had had the blessing of time to say goodbye in the way each of us needed to. As we spoke with Papa that morning, we were encouraged to hear the hope and peace in his voice. We joked about what foods we would eat when he was done and told him to go easy on the nurses.

We knew the recovery for this surgery would be longer than most of his previous operations. We would likely be unable to speak with him for at least a couple of days. We told him we would talk with him soon, and then we prayed. Many of our friends and family prayed along with us.

Several family members were with him along the way. In the pre-op room the morning of his surgery, he was talking less and less, slower and slower, quieter and weaker. He must be tired, they reasoned. He never slept well in the hospitals. He was fighting his fatigue, in and out of sleep, but he forced himself to slowly utter the words, one at a time, "If…"

Grandma filled in. "Let's not worry about that, Bud." (His nickname)

"If…," he insisted.

"Okay, if something happens," she suggested.

"Have…blessed…wonderful…life"

He was quiet for some time after, and the rest of the family passed the time. Suddenly Papa stiffened, opened his eyes wide, and said loudly, the clearest words he had uttered for hours, "Lord! Jesus!" Then he relaxed and closed his eyes again. He had never done something like that before.

They came to take him to the operating room not long after. Before the anesthesiologist took him, he said, "Now is the time to give hugs and kisses." Grandma went first, then Kelly, one of Papa's daughters. Kelly told Papa she loved him. Papa, still having trouble speaking, just said, "Love." It triggered something in Kelly, and she began to cry, overcome with fear this may be the last time she would see her father alive.

Just before taking Papa away for surgery, the anesthesiologist moved close to Kelly. It took a moment for her to notice he had been intently watching her with his bright, sparkling eyes. His expression somehow communicated deep empathy. He gently placed his hand on her forearm. With a kind and reassuring tone, he said,

"Don't worry, we're going to take really good care of him." She later described the experience felt wholly unique, different from any interaction she had ever had. He left her, she explained, with an inexplicable peace.

The operation finished more quickly than expected. Everything went smoothly. We thanked God. Papa, partially sedated, was semi-responsive after the surgery and was expected to sleep through the night.

In the early hours of the morning as Papa was sleeping, alarms blared. A flood of nurses into the room. They had to perform twenty-six minutes of chest compressions. After the chaos subsided and they stabilized Papa, the staff shared their grave concern that since he had gone so long without proper oxygen, Papa was at great risk for widespread, permanent brain damage. When we received the news, we prayed Papa's brain would be unharmed. *However, if he did have serious brain damage*, many of us prayed, *please take him home.* We knew that was what Papa wanted.

They took Papa for a brain scan and learned Papa had experienced several strokes. The damage was catastrophic, recovery impossible. He was gone. Only a shell remained.

Papa's final wishes were very clear. Through all of his brushes with death in the last year, he had considered every possibility and carefully composed instructions. Although Grandma still struggled knowing when to let his body go from life support, the important decisions had already been made. Eventually, she was able to say her final goodbye.

As we grieve, there will be many questions. Papa was still relatively young – why him? Why wouldn't God just heal him? Did we not pray enough? Was our faith not strong enough? Will Grandma be okay? Will she still be able to see God's unending love for her?

We have to remind ourselves over and over of the Biblical answers to these questions as our hearts adjust to what our heads know. Perhaps most importantly, we have to find God's goodness and blessing instead of focusing on where we feel He has failed us. Much of experiencing miracles is simply looking for them.

Papa defied the odds again and again. He lived over 8 years after his first major heart surgery. God's goodness through modern technology and expert doctors stretched Papa's life far longer than he would have lived if in the same situation only decades ago. God allowed Papa's heart to scar in just the right place to miraculously prevent its total rupture and keep him with us for another month and a half after the pseudoaneurysm. Through all of the hospital stays, Papa was able to encourage, inspire, and witness to countless hospital staff. Papa was able to say goodbye to all of his loved ones. He had arranged everything to make his passing as logistically smooth as possible for Grandma and the family. Grandma had time to adjust to the idea of life after Papa and talk with him at length about it. Although it would never be easy, she was as ready as she ever would be. Most importantly, Papa accepted Jesus before he died, and we all have the blessed assurance of knowing that.

Until we get to Heaven, we will never know exactly what happened and why, but Kelly believes Papa saw Jesus there in the pre-op room. Papa was scared, and Kelly believes Jesus visited Papa to reassure him and tell Papa that He would be taking him home. She also believes the anesthesiologist who comforted her right afterward may have been an angel confirming Papa's destination. At the very least, Kelly believes God spoke through the anesthesiologist to bring her peace.

A few hours after we learned of Papa's passing, my sister-in-law sent the family a photograph of a baseball player who had just hit a game-winning home run. He was rounding third with arms wide in celebration. As he approached home plate, his ecstatic teammates waited to embrace him. On every face in the photo, pure joy. The moment after the shutter: unrestrained elation.

She also sent this text message:
While we are so sad that we don't get to see him again until we join him in Heaven, I think it's such a great picture of what he received yesterday as he walked through the gates.

Later, Ryan added this context:
I just remembered when he hit that home run it was a grand slam when the Cubs were down by three. But also he was down to his last strike. It had never happened before.

Papa was certainly on his last strike. The circumstances were as dire as they could be, but there is one important difference: we always win when we are on God's team. I imagine the celebration is similar to the picture though – just with innumerably more teammates!

We must remember the best possible outcome for Papa is for him to run home to Jesus. That mercy is the greatest miracle Papa could ever receive. So we are celebrating Papa's miracle.

Papa in the aftermath of a snowball fight with his granddaughters

CHAPTER TWENTY

The Greatest Miracle

You may be reading this book because you need a miracle. Maybe you have been praying for one for years. Even if not, the question nearly everyone wants to ask is this: "How can I get a miracle?"

There is only one common denominator. There is only one ingredient all of these miracles have: God. As frustrating as it is, we do not get to decide when and how we get a miracle. There is no secret recipe. There are no magic words. It is God's prerogative to perform miracles. Ultimately, that is as it should be. God knows better than we do, as impossible as that is to understand in some situations.

There is, however, one thing we can do to encourage and recognize the miraculous in our lives: be close to Him. Think about it: who saw Jesus's miracles the most? *The people who were closest to Him.* If we get as close to Him as we can, though, we will realize the greatest gift bestowed by proximity to the God of the universe is not miracles to change our earthly situations. As Ashley discovered, the greatest gift we receive by knowing God is simply that: we get to know Him and be called a son or daughter of the Most High God.

By knowing Him, everything else shifts. We understand who we are and why we are here. We feel deeply, fully, unconditionally loved. We have hope and purpose.

Miracles are amazing, but they are bouquets and chocolates. They come and go. They are beautiful because they are transcendent and transient. Jesus made wine from water because the wedding had run out of wine. But guess what? Jesus's wine eventually ran out, too. When Jesus fed the five thousand, those same five thousand were hungry the next morning. After Jesus raised Lazarus from the dead, Lazarus eventually died again. A miracle to change your circumstances is temporary; your relationship with God is eternal, which brings us to the greatest miracle.

***

I imagine when God was creating the universe, He was distracted while composing the galaxies. His mind kept jumping ahead, imagining her reaction when the object of His affection saw His romantic gesture. He could not wait to hold her in His arms and love her forever.

Her initial reaction was perfect. She embraced His love, and they lived happily for some time, but her heart wandered. Even though God gave her perfection, she had free will, so she strayed. Nevertheless, God pursued. He reminded her over and over how much He loved her. He reminisced with her about the memories they had shared and how much better life was when they were together, but she was fickle.

He saved her life. She thanked Him and then aimlessly walked toward another cliff. He rearranged the sun and the stars for her. She thanked Him and then pursued someone else.

Through all of this, God simply wanted to love her and for her to love Him back. However, He had created a paradox: love cannot exist without choice, but choice cannot exist without rejection. Yet God persisted. He crafted a proposal, not because he needed her, because He wanted her. It is His very nature to love, and His love is limitless. The magnitude of His love shone through her brokenness and His relentless desire despite it.

There was only one way for God to have eternal relationship with the object of His affection.

To a God who has no limits, what is the greatest miracle? To the One who created the heavens and the Earth, what is the greatest gesture of adoration? What could He give, what could He pay that could demonstrate the desperation of His love?

The most spectacular manifestation of His love must come through sacrifice, but what could a God who has everything – who *created* everything – sacrifice?

The greatest miracle is this: while we were still sinners, Christ Jesus died for us. God sent His only Son to die on our behalf. Our imperfection demanded a perfect sacrifice to make it possible for us to be in eternal relationship with a perfect God. He does not need us, but He wants us, desperately. There is no grander gesture of love and sacrifice than what Christ did for us on the cross. Now, the Bible says, God sees His followers not in light of what they have done but in light of what Jesus did.

That is not the end, though. Jesus did not die for us so we would always remember Him. He resurrected Himself so we could always *be* with Him. He loves you, enough to move Heaven and Earth to create proposal after proposal for you. The God of the universe is bending down on one knee, looking you in the eye, and declaring His undying love for you – no, His *resurrecting* love for you. "Will you let me love you forever?"

But a proposal requires a response. The heavens are holding their collective breath. Will it be *yes*?

To say yes, just believe and pray this prayer: *Jesus, I believe you died to forgive my sins. Despite my sins and shortcomings, you made a grand gesture of love to propose to me at the cross. My answer is yes! I want to spend eternity with you. Come into my heart so we can spend eternity together! Amen.*

About the Author

Lee Freeman was born in Kansas City, Missouri, where he grew up in the "Historic Northeast." Apparently, "historic" was code for decrepit. It was a cesspool of prostitution, gang warfare, drugs, broken homes, and – interestingly enough – stray dogs.

At a young age, Lee realized the stark contrast between the loving, Christian atmosphere inside his home and the hellish chaos outside. His parents gave him many gifts during his upbringing, but the greatest was a Biblical worldview. Lee accepted Jesus at an early age, and although he is grossly imperfect and his life is full of challenges, he has never forsaken his faith.

After escaping the ghetto by immigrating to Loveland, Colorado, Lee grew up and became a high school English teacher. He teaches at the school he attended, where he also met his wife of eight years. They now live with their cat Quigley in a cute condo five minutes from their church, where they help lead worship together.

www.GenuineMiracles.com

Acknowledgments

First and foremost, I must thank God for giving me this calling. It has been some of the most rewarding work of my life, and I have seen so clearly that it is orchestrated and appointed by Him. I attribute all of the successes of this project to His guidance and blessing. I attribute any shortcomings to my persistent sinful nature, pride, ignorance, and many other failings. Despite my imperfections, though, I am eternally grateful He has saved me and calls me His own. His grace is sufficient to cover all of my flaws, and He is powerful enough to bless this project in spite of me.

Secondly, I must thank my incredible wife. She

has encouraged me, challenged me, and loved me selflessly throughout this project. More importantly, she has helped to point me to God throughout our life together. I could not ask for a better partner with whom to experience this adventure. Next to God, she is the strongest force helping me to look more like Jesus. My marriage to her is both the greatest blessing and the most important calling I have aside from my relationship with God.

Next, thank you to all my family and friends for your support. Although I often feel undeserving of your love and grace, I am so grateful for it. Without it, this project would be impossible.

My sincerest thanks to everyone who was willing to read through the manuscript, providing edits and feedback. This book is richer, more accurate, and more resonant because of your input.

Finally, thank you to each person who was willing to be interviewed, to host me, to coordinate, etc. Your courage, generosity, and vulnerability are inspiring, and they unite to make this project something truly profound.

To everyone who contributed in any way, may God grant you a special blessing for your willingness to be part of this work.

This book is not only the work of the author, it is the willingness of many, many people to contribute. It is the work of an incredible God. This book is a shared asset, an artifact of God's presence, power, and goodness in today's world.

Thank you for reading. It is my sincerest prayer that God has used this book to reveal His love and faithfulness to you. If this book encouraged you, would you consider giving it to someone else? People need to know that miracles are real, and they need to know the God who makes them!

A portion of all proceeds goes to Ordinary Nurses, a missionary nonprofit in Guatemala using nutrition, medicine, and education to love the rural people there and introduce them to Jesus. Remaining proceeds are used to share more miraculous stories with the world and spread God's love and hope to a world in such desperate need of both.

Top 6 Ways to Support This Ministry

1. Pray for us! Specifically:
    a) That God would use this ministry to reach lost people and help them to find salvation in Jesus
    b) That God would use this ministry to encourage and embolden existing believers
2. Tell us about your miracle, and be willing to be interviewed! Send your story to genuinemiracles@gmail.com
3. Give $3 or more per month to unlock exclusive benefits at www.patreon.com/genuinemiracles
4. Leave a positive review for the book on Amazon
5. Subscribe to the Genuine Miracles YouTube channel
6. Share our videos (liking and commenting helps, too!)

Your support allows us to

a) Go anywhere God leads us to find the most compelling stories
b) Publish more stories
c) Support Ordinary Nurses, a Guatemalan missionary organization

18195359R00133

Made in the USA
Middletown, DE
06 December 2018